Study Guide

# Worlds Together, Worlds Apart

SECOND EDITION

Volume 2

## THE MONGOL EMPIRE TO THE PRESENT

Chapters 10–21

# Worlds Together, Worlds Apart

SECOND EDITION

## Volume 2

## THE MONGOL EMPIRE TO THE PRESENT

Chapters 10–21

ROBERT TIGNOR • JEREMY ADELMAN • STEPHEN ARON • PETER BROWN • BENJAMIN ELMAN • STEPHEN KOTKIN • XINRU LIU • SUZANNE MARCHAND • HOLLY PITTMAN • GYAN PRAKASH • BRENT D. SHAW • MICHAEL TSIN

*Michael G. Murdock*

BRIGHAM YOUNG UNIVERSITY–HAWAII

 W • W • NORTON & COMPANY • NEW YORK • LONDON

**ISBN 978-0-393-93207-2 (pbk.)**

W. W. Norton & Company, Inc., 500 Fifth Avenue, New York, NY 10110
www.wwnorton.com

W. W. Norton & Company Ltd., Castle House, 75/76 Wells Street, London W1T 3QT

1 2 3 4 5 6 7 8 9 0

# CONTENTS

# PREFACE

This study guide has been specifically designed to supplement the study and teaching of world history as presented in *Worlds Together, Worlds Apart: A History of the World from the Beginnings of Humankind to the Present*. Its primary purpose is make world history come alive by offering both students and teachers different ways to grapple with the material. To fulfill this task, each chapter has been organized into the following sections:

*Chapter Objectives* This short section identifies the key themes and foci of each specific chapter of the *Worlds Together, Worlds Apart* text.

*Chapter Outline, Chronology, and Summary* Here, text chapter material is synthesized and abbreviated. Teachers may use this section as a quick review of chapters before beginning their lecture. Students may use it to test their understanding by examining the main ideas of the chapter. Note that the headings in this section parallel those of the text chapters so that teachers and students can quickly reference the text for a fuller picture and more detail.

*Questions for Class Discussion* This section presents five open-ended, discussion-related questions that capture the essence and major themes of each text chapter. Teachers may use the questions to stimulate thought in class or as essay questions on an exam. Students may use them as challenging exercises to enhance their own thinking about world history and to explore new ways of analyzing what they've learned.

*Multiple-Choice Questions* The multiple-choice questions presented in this section can be used by teachers to examine student knowledge. The questions are not, however, mere measures of trivia but seek to capture important concepts or developments.

*Map Exercise* The map exercises provide students and teachers alike with tactile, exploratory, and creative experiences designed to augment analytical skills. These questions and exercises can be used as term projects or short paper topics. To answer the questions, students are compelled to seek new information and stretch their thinking rather than simply regurgitating information. As geographical and historical knowledge expands, the map exercises allow students to employ that knowledge in new interpretive ways.

*Keywords* This section identifies most of the new vocabulary words encountered in each of the *Worlds Together, Worlds Apart* chapters. Teachers may use these lists to help prepare for their lectures, or they can employ the terms to test the knowledge base of their students. Students can use the lists as a study guide of major events and vocabulary words.

## ACKNOWLEDGMENTS

I would like to thank Matthew Arnold for input and his gracious offer to let me work on this wonderful advance in the study of world history.

# Worlds Together, Worlds Apart

SECOND EDITION

Volume 2

THE MONGOL EMPIRE TO THE PRESENT

Chapters 10–21

# CHAPTER 10 | Becoming "The World," 1000–1300 CE

## CHAPTER OBJECTIVES

- To explain the reasons behind the explosion of interregional contact and trade and its impact on the various regions of the world.
- To understand the emergence of large regions with definable parts, shared cultures, and political structures, even as the world was being connected by long-distance trade.

## CHAPTER OUTLINE, CHRONOLOGY, AND SUMMARY

At the beginning of the new millennium, four distinct cultural and political regions dominated the Afro-Eurasian world: Chinese, Indian, Islamic, and European. Two main trends characterized this period: a maritime revolution that increased interregional commercial contact, and the sharpening of cultural, religious, and political distinctions in the Afro-Eurasian world. Although isolated from these main trends, societies in the Americas underwent a similar process of increased interregional contact. In the thirteenth century, nomadic Mongol invaders conquered a large part of Afro-Eurasia, capping this era of interregional contact with a short-lived layer of political integration.

## A Globe of Regional Worlds

The period from 1000 to 1300 witnessed tremendous population growth, increasing cross-cultural contact, interregional trade, and the creation of strong militarized states. These trends affected populations around the globe. At the end of the period, however, regions and states had not become more alike as a result of increased contact, growing trade, and common political experiences. In fact, the sense of differ-

ence and apartness became more deeply ingrained in each region's culture, leading toward a sense of distinct cultural identities such as "Europe" or "China" and bringing the world closer to contemporary regional identities.

## Commercial Connections

Trade began to grow faster in this period. Increased trade across regions led to cross-cultural contact and continued population growth. Increased trade and population growth brought about commercial cities that served as centers of long-distance trade. Trade grew as a result of earlier developments in agriculture and commerce as well as inventions and improvements in areas such as shipbuilding.

### REVOLUTIONS AT SEA

Long-distance trade increasingly took place over sea routes rather than land routes from 1000 to 1300. Several technological improvements and commercial changes helped make sea routes safer and more profitable than land routes. For example, Chinese sailors began using the needle compass to help them navigate during cloudy weather and on the open seas. Use of the compass soon spread through Southeast Asia and India. The long-term shift toward sea routes and away from land routes brought new connections between regions as well as new divisions.

### COMMERCIAL CONTACTS

Changes in world agriculture during this period were also gradual and built on developments from earlier periods. Before the year 1000, farmers had invested in and explored long-term irrigation projects, improvements in grain crops, new grasses for fodder, and planting in new regions. These developments helped to create surpluses of staple goods such as rice, linen, and cotton textiles. These goods were increasingly transported long distances in ships, since they offered greater capacity than land caravans and lower operating costs. Ships could also carry large, heavy, fragile items for trade.

### GLOBAL COMMERCIAL HUBS

Commercial cities, or entrepôts, developed as a result of long-distance maritime trade. Three places served as major centers or anchorages of maritime trade: Cairo-Fustat in the west; Quanzhou in the east; and Quilon in the Indian peninsula. In each case, the city benefited from powerful rulers who took steps to facilitate trade in order to profit from it.

### THE EGYPTIAN ANCHORAGE

Cairo and Alexandria served as the center of trade between Europe and the Indian Ocean. Trading firms in these cities formed around families, each practicing its own religion. Trade between the firms thus brought trade across religions. Firms in Cairo and Alexandria traded luxury items such as silks; local Mediterranean goods such as olive oil; staples and raw materials such as timber; and novelty items such as paper and books. Islamic leaders in the area protected merchants with regular convoys and permitted Muslim merchants to form partnerships so that loans and investments would remain profitable without violating Islamic law.

### THE ANCHORAGE OF QUANZHOU

In Quanzhou, the Song government created offices that served in effect as a customs agency, charging taxes and overseeing and protecting merchants, ships, cargo, and sailors. Both Chinese and foreign traders and sailors sought protection from a local goddess and participated in an annual ritual led by the governor of Quanzhou to summon favorable winds. Sailors leaving Quanzhou and arriving there used large flat-bottomed ships called junks. These ships were large enough to carry as many as 500 sailors. Foreign traders at Quanzhou included Arabs, Persians, Jews, and Indians. Foreign merchant families sometimes stayed in Quanzhou for long periods. They lived throughout the city and practiced their own religions.

### THE TIP OF INDIA

In south India, the Chola dynasty supported and protected maritime trade around the southwest coast of India and eastward as far as the Melakan Strait. The southwest coast, especially Quilon, became a center of trade between China and the Mediterranean. Luxury items of all kinds were traded east and west, including silks, horses, spices, and textiles. Merchant families settling in trading hubs like Quilon often had commercial and family ties in other hubs as well, helping them reach across cultures.

## Regions Together, Regions Apart

Long-distance trade brought peoples and cultures into contact with more intensity than ever before. In large commercial cities, traders crossed cultural and religious boundaries on a regular basis to complete their transactions, creating economic and political organizations that accommodated the commercial needs of different regions—in effect, bringing the world closer together. Yet this closer contact also highlighted the differences between cultures and regions.

### SUB-SAHARAN AFRICA COMES TOGETHER

Beginning around 1000 CE, economic and cultural contacts with outside areas spread through sub-Saharan Africa. In earlier periods, geographic barriers had deterred interregional trade. During this period, long-distance and interregional trade brought cultural, religious, and economic exchanges with other regions within Africa and other parts of the world.

### WEST AFRICA AND MANDE-SPEAKING PEOPLES

A mobile, adaptable group who spoke similar languages and shared a culture, created trading networks that linked far-flung regions, and dominated West Africa. This group, the Mande-speaking people, formed different types of governments and societies in the different regions of West Africa, including small-scale societies, centralized governments, and sacred kingships. The Mande established trading routes and trading centers through the interior to the Atlantic and controlled much of the trade across the Sahara. The Sahara trade featured coveted items such as salt, as well as gold and slaves.

### THE EMPIRE OF MALI

The Empire of Mali, founded by Mande-speaking groups, flourished from the first half of the twelfth century until the fifteenth. Known for its wealth and for rulers like Mansa Musa, the Islamic empire included two of the largest cities in West Africa: Jenne and Timbuktu. Both were thriving commercial entrepôts serving interregional trade routes. Timbuktu was also a religious and intellectual center for Muslim scholars.

### EAST AFRICA AND THE INDIAN OCEAN

Cities in eastern and southern Africa became central parts of the Indian Ocean trade. Swahili merchants in cities like Kilwa and Mogadishu traded goods from the African interior for goods from the Arabian peninsula and the west coast of India. Gold mined in the East African highlands by the Shona people offered the most attractive profits for Swahili merchants. The island of Madagascar was also a key commercial hub in the Indian Ocean trade. Its location off East Africa brought multiple cultures and economies into contact from around the Indian Ocean, bringing to Madagascar a fusion of cultures as well as commerce.

THE TRANS-SAHARAN AND INDIAN OCEAN SLAVE TRADE

Slaves were a valuable and significant part of the interregional trade across the Mediterranean and Indian Ocean, with millions of Africans traded during this period. Slavery in the world of the Mediterranean and the Indian Ocean differed from the type of slavery prevalent through the Americas a few centuries later. The *Quran* taught that slaves should be treated with kindness and generosity. Slaves were assigned to a variety of roles, including service in the military, working as sailors or domestic servants, serving as concubines to rulers, and in certain cultures working as plantation laborers. Although slavery was common, local and regional economies were not founded on its basis.

ISLAM IN A TIME OF INSTABILITY

The Islamic empire during this period also experienced greater prosperity based on interregional trade. Indeed, Muslim merchants centered in the Islamic Middle East helped to establish the region as another "core" region in the world. The region's wealth increasingly came from the expanding Afro-Eurasian trade networks. These commercial networks provided a path for converting local urban and peasant populations in the region to Islam. Sufi orders helped bring together local religious traditions and the new faith, making Islam more adaptable as it grew. Yet the growth of Islam did not bring local populations together under a common ruler. Instead, the Islamic region was subject to a series of defeats by outsiders.

AFRO-EURASIAN MERCHANTS

Long-distance merchants from diverse ethnic backgrounds established large commercial networks. These networks often centered in Southwest Asia due to its location at the center of Afro-Eurasia. Muslim long-distance merchants relied on a shared Islamic culture, Arabic language, and Islamic law to help them negotiate trade arrangements that reached across ethnic lines or regions. Trade arrangements were based on contracts, partnerships, and other commercial structures that were enforced through local religious courts. Because these trade arrangements were so vital to conducting long-distance trade, those who violated agreements were severely punished by the merchant community.

DIVERSITY AND UNIFORMITY IN ISLAM

The Islamic empire in this period was characterized by acceptance of religious minorities as long as the minorities accepted Islam's ultimate political rule through payment of a special tax and respect for Islamic rulers. Religious minorities could practice their own religions, settle their own disputes, and participate in the economy. Religious diversity existed even within Islam, as seen in the Sufi brotherhoods that flourished in this period. This general tolerance helped accommodate traders from around the world who sought to establish business networks in the Islamic empire. Religious tensions arose within the Islamic empire at times, especially with the Christian minorities in the frontier areas as European Christians at times pressed against Muslim borders.

POLITICAL INTEGRATION AND DISINTEGRATION 1050–1300 CE

During the period from 1050 to 1300, no single ethnic or political group was strong enough to hold sway over the Islamic core area. Shiite strongholds in Egypt and Baghdad fell to Sunni Muslims. In the east, the old Abbasid empire was in the hands of a series of caliphs without real political or religious influence. The center was led by non-Arabs. The west was ruled by Arabs, but non-Arab Berbers represented an important minority. The Islamic faith was expanding both within this region and outside its borders, but politics were fractured within the Islamic core.

WHAT IS ISLAM?

The period from 1000 to 1300 was critical to the evolution of Islam. By 1300, Islam was no longer a religion of Arab desert nomads, and Arabic was no longer its only language. Jerusalem and Baghdad were no longer its only cultural capitals. The Sufi brotherhoods helped convert urban populations and peasants throughout Afro-Eurasia. Important Islamic cities and universities developed in several areas, where Muslims worshiped in Persian and Turkish, although Arabic remained the dominant language of Islam. This heterogeneity within Islam reflected the ability of the Sufi brotherhoods to reach out to ordinary people in the cities and rural areas. The *ulama* spoke to the educated and scholarly classes through the *sharia*. By 1300, Islam had become the people's faith.

## India Up for Grabs

India's location at the crossroads of interregional commercial routes led to tremendous cultural diversity within the context of Hinduism. Similar to the Islamic core, however, there was little political integration within India. With the second largest population in Afro-Eurasia and a prosperous economy, India was divided into areas controlled by local rajas. When Islamic Turks invaded from the north around 1000, the rajas could not resist. The Turkish invaders relied on the local rajas, who forged alliances with Brahman groups, giving them land in return for recognition of the rajas' ancestry and status. These alliances benefited both the Brahmanic groups and the rajas, increasing their agricultural income and providing for support for Sanskrit culture by the rajas.

INVASIONS AND CONSOLIDATIONS

Turkish invasions continued through the eleventh and twelfth centuries, gradually overcoming the local rulers and divided kingdoms all the way to the lower Ganges valley. Turkish warlords generally practiced tolerance of existing political structures and cultural diversity. They also brought Turkish customs and built Islamic mosques and libraries in the conquered areas. In northern India, the powerful Turkish Muslim regime (called the Delhi Sultanate) devoted its attention to political integration and the rich agriculture of the region, allowing commercial life on the coast to develop autonomously. As a result, Persian traders settled near modern-day Bombay, and Arab traders dominated the Malabar coast to the south.

### WHAT IS INDIA?

India's cultural development during this period continued the pattern of assimilation and diversity that had characterized earlier periods. Turkish Muslim invaders from the north cooperated with Indian political leaders, accepting cultural diversity as long as local populations paid their taxes. However, the Turks continued to practice Islam, retained their distinctive style of dress, and employed Persian as the language of the court and administration. Hindu subjects continued to practice the Hindu faith, followed caste regulations, and spoke local languages.

Turkish sultans erected fortresses and palaces in Delhi built by local workers and foreign artisans. These palaces and fortresses became prosperous cities. As they completed these buildings, local workers and foreign artisans learned techniques and crafts from each other, leading to continued cultural blending.

Hinduism and Islam flourished under the Turkish sultans, while Buddhism gradually diminished. Muslim sultans granted lands to Islamic scholars and Sufi saints, just as the Hindu rajas had granted lands to Brahman groups. Muslim scholars and saints attracted followers, and Islam spread throughout Delhi. Hinduism had already absorbed many Buddhist beliefs and practices. With the arrival of more Turkish invaders in the thirteenth century, many Buddhist scholars left Delhi and settled in Tibet. Buddhist followers in India, left with a Muslim regime and little spiritual leadership, gradually turned to Hinduism or converted to Islam.

## Song China

With the end of the Tang dynasty in 907, China splintered into regional kingdoms. After decades of fragmentation, the Song dynasty reunified China by conquering all seven major regions by 1000, beginning three centuries of Song rule. The Song government enjoyed prosperity and stability within most of the empire, maintaining China's role as the driving force behind Afro-Eurasian economic growth during this period. However, the Song dynasty continually faced encroachments and invasions from the north, losing control of northern China in 1127 and then losing their southern base to the Mongols in 1276.

### A CHINESE COMMERCIAL REVOLUTION

The prosperity of the Song period was founded on improvements in agriculture, especially the use of the iron plow. With iron plows and farm animals, new areas could be cultivated and crop production, particularly rice, soared. More food was then available to feed a growing population. Other improvements and inventions of the Song period included the development of gunpowder, canons, and other explosive devices; lighter, stronger porcelains; and increased production of clothing and crafts.

In order to trade all these manufactured goods and agricultural products, merchants needed access to large amounts of currency. The Song government significantly increased its production of metal currency, but demand still outpaced supply, contributing to increased demand for gold from East Africa. Soon merchants began to use printed paper certificates to promise payments. The use of paper currency spread, replacing coins by the thirteenth century. The Song government also depended on paper currency, and when it needed more funds, the government printed more money. This habit contributed to spiraling inflation, which eventually destabilized the Song government.

### NEW ELITES

During the Song period, civilian values increasingly dominated society. These values were reflected in the classic texts of Confucianism that candidates for civil service studied. The Song dynasty continued to administer civil service examinations, with the emperor serving as the final examiner. The civil officials who passed the exams took an oath of allegiance to the Song emperor. They became the new ruling elite, replacing the hereditary ruling class of aristocratic families from earlier periods. As a result, Song society was governed by a new class of scholar-officials who formed the central bureaucracy.

### NEGOTIATING WITH NEIGHBORS

The Song dynasty, located in the core of greater China, faced continual pressures from nomadic societies located on its northern borders. These nomadic societies adapted Chinese military techniques and inventions, often using them successfully against Song armies on the borders. Song emperors negotiated peace terms with gifts and generous trade agreements. When the government spent its money negotiating peace terms, Song officials simply printed more paper money. As runaway inflation inevitably developed, economic instability combined with military weakness, increasing the vulnerability of the Song government.

### WHAT IS CHINA?

Constant contacts with outsiders ended up strengthening the difference that the Han Chinese felt. The Han's northern homeland fell to nomadic societies during this period. As the Han were driven southward, they became more conscious of differences between their own social values and traditions and the values and traditions of outsiders. The Han considered themselves the true Chinese, with a society based on farming, education, and literacy, and living according to traditional civilian values. The Han called outsiders "barbarians" who lived in nomadic warrior societies, creating stereotypes that persisted despite long periods of peaceful coexistence and interchange.

China's print culture expanded rapidly during this period, easily surpassing the print resources of other Afro-Eurasian societies. The Song government published books, medical texts, and calendars. Private publishers printed Confucian classics, histories, and other literature used in the civil service examinations, as well as Buddhist publications. China's print culture spread to Korea, where movable metal type was developed in 1234.

## China's Neighbors, 1000–1300

China's wealth and large population meant that its cultural and economic influence extended across Afro-Eurasia and was especially strong among its neighbors. Local elites in Korea, Japan, and Southeast Asian states bought luxury items from Chinese merchants, selling staple goods to Chinese cities along the coast. Along with the commercial goods, local elites acquired a taste for Chinese religion, technology, and culture.

### THE RISE OF WARRIORS IN JAPAN

With China's increasing economic and political strength, neighboring states faced a choice: they could overcome internal divisions and build solid governments to preserve some autonomy, or they could maintain weak or fractured systems and risk Chinese cultural and economic domination. In Japan, multiple sources of power existed in an atmosphere of intrigue. In the capital city, court nobles began claiming that they were the sacred emperor's protector, ruling in his name. Then warrior factions began adopting the same role, seizing the emperor's throne as a symbol of his power and calling themselves the emperor's protector.

Outside the capital, large private estates held sway with over half of Japan's rice land in the hands of large estates by 1100. Wealth, influence, and power shifted to the provinces under the protection of trained warriors, expert horsemen who defended private estates. These local warriors, called shoguns, helped to bridge the divide between the aristocracy in the capital and the landowners of the provinces. Shoguns and the aristocracy formed alliances by any way necessary to gain power.

The Kamakura shoguns finally brought more stability to Japan through a system of alliances with local officials and military commanders. The Kamakura, "protectors" of the emperor in the capital city, established alliances strong enough to protect Japan from Mongol invasion in the late thirteenth century. The system of shogunate military government under the figurehead of the emperor remained intact until 1868.

### THE CULTURAL MOSAIC OF SOUTHEAST ASIA

Southeast Asia resembled India in the sense of serving as a crossroads of trade routes across Afro-Eurasia. Like the commercial cities on the Indian coast, trading ports and busy harbors in Southeast Asia brought together merchants and sailors from China, India, the Islamic empire, and local polities. Merchants and sailors spent several months at ports such as Melaka, selling their goods and buying a new cargo while waiting for seasonal shifts in the monsoon winds. In contrast to India, the population of Southeast Asia remained relatively low, and the area retained much of its island culture.

Some groups on the Southeast Asian mainland flourished as a result of contact and trade with China and India. The Thai, Vietnamese, and Burmese peoples developed large populations. The Cambodian, Burmese, and Thai peoples established powerful polities along mainland river basins. Several Buddhist kingdoms developed between China and India. Each group showed the cultural and economic reach of China and India in its particular blend of local traditions with outside influences. The temples of Angkor in the Khmer empire exemplify the influence of Indian culture on a bordering state.

## Christian Europe

A different culture began to develop in the area known as Europe, occupying the far western corner of the Eurasian land mass. Relatively underpopulated in comparison to India and China, Europe experienced rapid population growth in the period up to the early fourteenth century. In the absence of a large unifying empire, politics in this area became increasingly localized, even as a "European" identity began to take shape.

### A WORLD OF KNIGHTS

A warrior class or aristocracy emerged with increased power in the aftermath of the collapse of the Carolingian empire and Viking invasions in northern Europe. This warrior aristocracy succeeded in subjugating the peasantry, creating a system known as "feudalism," where they controlled peasants' lives and labor. Rapid population growth helped northern Europe emerge from the shadows of the Mediterranean world, while a transformation in agricultural productivity brought this region into the world of global trade.

### EASTERN EUROPE

The large, open spaces of eastern Europe provided a haven for peasants seeking to escape feudalism. Local elites wishing to adopt the lifestyles of their western European counterparts were able to attract peasant migrants with the promise of greater freedoms than they had in the west.

### THE RUSSIAN LANDS

Farther to the east, the vast lands of Russia served as the border between Europe and the steppes of Afro-Eurasia. The city of Kiev emerged as a commercial crossroads that looked southward to Byzantium for religious, political, and cultural inspiration. To the north and northeast, smaller replicas of Kiev served as commercial oases and outposts of Orthodox Christianity.

### WHAT IS CHRISTIAN EUROPE?

Between 1000 and 1300, European Christianity was transformed from a religion of monks to a mass faith. Churches became an integral part of the numerous villages that were founded as part of the internal colonization of western Europe. The clergy was given jurisdiction over areas such as marriage and divorce that were previously considered to be private, family matters. Through the efforts of men like Francis of Assisi, Christian practices came to be seen as part of daily life.

## UNIVERSITIES AND INTELLECTUALS

Universities emerged as the center where communities of scholars could advance learning in relative freedom from the interference of secular or religious authorities. In cities like Paris, universities became centers for the absorption and discussion of Arab learning. Scholars also endeavored to provide intellectual support for the idea of Christianity as a dominant religion. Based on a thriving Christianity, by 1300, Europe had greater cultural unity than before, even as it became a more intolerant place for non-Christians.

## TRADERS AND WARRIORS

Led by the powerful trading hubs of Venice and Genoa, western European commercial activity reached outward to the Mediterranean and beyond. This brought them into conflict with long-established but declining powers such as the Byzantine Empire. Genoese sailors were particularly active in linking the Mediterranean with European Atlantic ports as far north as Flanders, and in mapping the West African coast.

## CRUSADERS

The first of four "crusades" began in 1095 with an appeal to warrior nobles from Pope Urban II to free Jerusalem from Muslim rule. Although highly publicized in the West, the Crusades had little impact on the Muslim Middle East. The Frankish kingdoms in the area were only temporary. Crusaders captured Jerusalem and established the Kingdom of Jerusalem, but in 1187, Christian armies were decisively defeated by Saladin's troops. Of more lasting importance was the deterioration of living conditions for the numerous non-Western Christians living in areas like Egypt and Syria. Ironically, Constantinople was among the victims of the crusades, as the city was sacked and captured by Frankish armies in 1204.

Christian expansionism was more successful in other areas. In Spain the northern Christian kingdoms gradually pushed back the frontiers of Muslim Spain, capturing Toledo in 1061 and Seville in 1248. Sicily, a wealthy and strategic island, was captured from the Muslims in 1091. These events were more decisive than the Crusades in tilting the balance of power between Christians and Muslims in the Mediterranean world.

## The Americas

The Americas remained isolated from the communications revolution that altered the Afro-Eurasian world in these centuries. However, internal changes in the fields of commerce and communication had a similar impact, bringing various people of the Americas into closer contact.

## ANDEAN STATES

South America's first empire, the Chimu Empire, developed in the eleventh century along the Moche Valley near the Pacific Ocean in modern-day Peru. The Chimu incorporated various ecological zones to create a commercialized agricultural state that survived until the Inca conquest in the 1460s. Advanced irrigation systems, maintained by a well-trained bureaucracy, allowed the Chimu to create a series of oases along the arid Pacific coast. At the center of the empire was the sprawling walled city of Chan Chan with a population of about thirty thousand people, featuring opulent palaces and treasure houses for cloth and objects of silver and gold.

Another powerful urban state, Tiwanaku, developed in the arid Andean highlands near the shores of Lake Titicaca. Less powerful and wealthy than the Chimu Empire, Tiwanaku relied on long-distance trade between the highlands, low-lying semitropical valleys, and the Pacific coast.

## NORTH AMERICAN CONNECTIONS

In Mesoamerica, the Toltecs filled the vacuum left by the fall of Teotihuacán in the valley of Central Mexico. Drawing from a base of refugees and migrant farmers, the Toltecs relied on the valley's rich agricultural production, while maintaining existing trade routes that reached out to the Gulf of Mexico, the Pacific Ocean, and the Central American lowlands. The Toltec capital of Tula grew rapidly as a commercial, political, and ceremonial center, reaching a population of 60,000 at the peak of its power. Influences of previous Mesoamerican civilizations were evident in the city's impressive architecture and monumental public works.

Farther to the north, other smaller urban trading hubs developed in North America. The largest of these hubs was in Cahokia, best known for its large earth mounds that served as places of spiritual worship. Located along the Mississippi River, Cahokia became a center for regional and long-distance trade, drawing goods from the Appalachian Mountains, the Gulf of Mexico, and the upper Great Lakes. Cahokia's success placed great stress on its environment, and by 1350 the city had declined and almost disappeared.

## The Mongol Transformation of Afro-Eurasia

Maritime commerce greatly transformed the Afro-Eurasian world during these centuries. But the next major transformation was initiated by nomadic conquerors from the inner regions of Afro-Eurasia—the Mongols. Beginning in 1206, Chinggis Khan and his descendants led a series of conquests that brought China, Korea, Central Asia, Persia, the caliphate of Baghdad, and the Russian principalities under direct or indirect rule by Mongols.

## MONGOLS IN CHINA

The Mongol conquest of China was begun by Chinggis Khan and completed decades later by his grandson, Kubilai. The north fell quickly, but the conquest of southern China was not completed until 1280. The Mongol conquests particularly impacted northern China, which saw a significant decline in population and economic production. Kubilai established the Yuan dynasty and ruled China from his new capital in Dadu (present-day Beijing). The Mongols also conquered Korea, but two naval invasions of Japan were unsuccessful. The Mongols did not destroy urbanized Chinese ways. Instead a new heterogeneous elite of diverse Afro-Eurasian peoples superimposed itself on Han Chinese elites.

## MONGOL REVERBERATIONS IN SOUTHEAST ASIA

Aftershocks of the Mongol conquest of China were felt throughout Southeast Asia. As part of the attempt to conquer southern reaches of the Song state, Mongol armies conquered the states of Dali and Pyu in neighboring Yunnan and Burma. Territories that had enjoyed autonomy from earlier Chinese dynasties were annexed to China by new Mongol rulers. A failed naval expedition to Java marked the limits of Mongol expansion.

## THE FALL OF BAGHDAD

The Mongol attack on the Islamic world was led by Hulagu Khan, another grandson of Chinggis Khan. The great prize was the city of Baghdad, even if its power over the Islamic world had greatly declined. An army of 200,000 captured the city with little difficulty, but exercised great ruthlessness. Contemporary accounts describe a massacre of immense proportions. Mongol armies rolled farther west into Syria until stopped by Egyptian Mamluk forces in 1261.

## QUESTIONS FOR CLASS DISCUSSION

1. What role did commercial hubs such as Cairo, Quanzhou, and Quilon play in promoting interregional trade during this period?
2. How did the activities of Muslim merchants contribute to the emergence of the Islamic world as one of the "core" regions in this period?
3. What were the strengths and weaknesses of Song China?
4. How were commercial and political developments in the Americas similar to and different from those that took place in the Afro-Eurasian world during this period?
5. How did the Mongols succeed in conquering a large part of the Afro-Eurasian world in the thirteenth century?

## MULTIPLE-CHOICE QUESTIONS

1. Which of the following did *not* contribute to the maritime revolution that facilitated the growth of long-distance trade?
   a. improved navigational aids such as the needle compass
   b. refinements in shipbuilding
   c. better mapmaking
   d. lack of protection from political authorities
   e. breakthroughs in commercial laws and accounting practices

2. The four major cultural regions of the Afro-Eurasian world between 1000 and 1300 were
   a. Korea, Japan, Persia, and Egypt.
   b. China, India, Europe, and the Islamic world.
   c. China, India, Turkey, and Egypt.
   d. India, Japan, Sub-Saharan Africa and Europe.
   e. China, southeast Asia, Europe, and the Islamic world.

3. The three leading global "entrepôts" or hubs of maritime trade of this period were
   a. Cairo, Timbuktu, and Kiev.
   b. Quanzhou, Constantinople, and Mogadishu.
   c. Cairo, Quanzhou, and Quilon.
   d. Quilon, Kiev, and Kilwa.
   e. Cairo, Quanzhou, and Mogadishu.

4. To which African political unit do the following terms—*Sundiata*, Mansa Musa, Timbuktu—correspond?
   a. the kingdom of Ghana
   b. the Muslim state of Songhai
   c. Great Zimbabwe
   d. the Empire of Mali
   e. the East African city-states on the Indian Ocean

5. The general attitude of Islamic rulers toward religious minorities was characterized by
   a. acceptance of religious minorities as long they accepted Islam's ultimate political hegemony.
   b. conversion efforts of non-Muslims by the *ulama*.
   c. lack of concern with the activities of Christians in borderland regions.
   d. persecution of all non-Muslim religious groups.
   e. privileged treatment of minorities who spoke Arabic.

6. The Turkish invasions of India
   a. made Islam the sole, dominant religion of India.
   b. added an Islamic layer to India's cultural mosaic.
   c. destroyed the power of local rajas.
   d. inaugurated a period of inward-looking stagnation.
   e. led to a Buddhist revival inside India.

7. Which of the following was *not* a feature of Song China?
   a. the development of gunpowder
   b. several centuries of stability and splendor
   c. large-scale production of manufactured goods for consumption and export
   d. better tools for agriculture
   e. aggressive diplomacy based on military power

8. Which of the following was *not* a feature of Japanese society during this period?
   a. the presence of multiple sources of power
   b. an emperor with purely symbolic power
   c. the emergence of shoguns who bridged the divide between local landowners and military commanders
   d. fear of Chinese culture
   e. provincial elites with little influence in the Japanese power structure

9. The cultural mosaic that characterized Southeast Asia in the period between 1000 and 1300 was a product of
   a. its geographical location at the crossroads that connected China with Asia and Africa.
   b. spillover from heavily populated regions of China and India.
   c. the presence of Hinduism, Buddhism, and Islam as major religions in the area.
   d. the ability of local peoples (Thai, Vietnamese, and Burmese) to strengthen their cultures by selectively adapting features of Indian and Chinese culture.
   e. all of the above

10. Which of the following did *not* contribute to the development of Europe's Christian identity?
    a. the transfer of jurisdiction over family matters to the clergy
    b. the founding of villages with parish churches across western Europe
    c. the continued emphasis on Christianity as a religion of monks
    d. the rise of universities
    e. the construction of monumental cathedrals

11. A borderland Christianity that looked to Byzantium for spiritual, cultural, and architectural inspiration developed in
    a. Poland.
    b. Northern Germany.
    c. Hungary.
    d. Sicily.
    e. Russia.

12. The principal long-term effect of the Crusades was
    a. to heal the rift between the eastern and western churches of the Christian world.
    b. a long-lasting European presence in Southwest Asia.
    c. the revitalization of the Byzantine Empire.
    d. deteriorating conditions for non-Western Christians in the Muslim world.
    e. the Christianization of Africa.

13. Between 1000 and 1300 strong commercial expansionist impulses were seen in all of the following societies of the Americas *except*
    a. the Chimu Empire.
    b. the Toltecs.
    c. Tiwanaku.
    d. the Incas.
    e. Cahokia.

14. The people known as the Toltecs
    a. filled the vacuum left by the decline of the city of Teotihuacán in Central Mexico.
    b. had their capital at Tula, which at the height of its power had close to 60,000 inhabitants.
    c. were formed from the combination of refugees from the south and farmers from the north.

d. produced enough food to satisfy their needs.
e. all of the above

15. Which of the following territories was *not* affected by the Mongol conquests of the thirteenth century?
    a. China
    b. Korea
    c. Egypt
    d. Persia
    e. Afghanistan

## MAP EXERCISE

Looking at a map of the globe, locate the four major cultural regions of the Afro-Eurasian world. Draw the major trade routes that pass through commercial centers in each region.

## KEYWORDS

needle compass
entrepôts
junks
Mande
sacred kingships
griot
Sufi brotherhoods
Delhi Sultanate
Song dynasty
gunpowder
Song porcelain
flying cash
civil service examinations
Han Chinese
barbarians
Heian period
shoguns
*Tale of Genji*
Khmers
Angkor Wat
Melaka
feudalism

"Little Europes"
Kiev
tsar/czar
universitas
Genoa
Crusades
Kingdom of Jerusalem
sack of Constantinople
erangi
Reconquista
Chimu Empire
the Moche
Chan Chan
Tiwanaku
Toltecs
Tula
Cahokia
"mound people"
Yuan dynasty
Hangzhou
semu

## ANSWERS TO MULTIPLE-CHOICE QUESTIONS

1. d
2. b
3. c
4. d
5. a
6. b
7. e
8. e
9. e
10. c
11. e
12. d
13. d
14. e
15. c

# CHAPTER 11 | Crises and Recovery in Afro-Eurasia, 1300s–1500s

## CHAPTER OBJECTIVES

- To identify and trace the rise of major new powers in Afro-Eurasia after the Mongol invasions and Black Death decimated existing polities
- To explain the growth of trade between these new empires or kingdoms and the rise of their cultural prominence

## CHAPTER OUTLINE, CHRONOLOGY, AND SUMMARY

Mongol invasions brought devastation beyond that of their armies. They also introduced the bubonic plague. Following Mongol armies and trade routes, the disease spread throughout Afro-Eurasia, resulting in tremendous destruction. Trading hubs, now filled with the dead and dying, suffered as interaction and population declined. During the fourteenth and fifteenth centuries, Afro-Eurasians rebounded with new polities and dynasties to replace those destroyed by the Mongols and the Black Death.

### Collapse and Integration

Many people assumed the Black Death to be God's punishment. Disruption and falling populations weakened political structures but helped others consolidate and centralize power.

THE BLACK DEATH

The disease involved a number of strains that commonly killed 25 to 50 percent of local populations. While climate changes may have contributed to the disease's spread, it was the Mongol invasions that dispersed it to China and other points around Afro-Eurasia before it began following trade routes to Italy. Reaching European soil, the disease infected rats before killing people. In China an estimated 40 million people perished. Food supplies dropped since the dead and sick could not farm. Cities, with dense populations, lost as much as two thirds of their population.

REBUILDING STATES

In the late fourteenth century, Afro-Eurasians began to rebuild devastated polities and disrupted trade networks. Most of these new polities were based on hereditary ruling families that claimed divine support, established clear rules of succession, built armies, and formed alliances with other states through marriage. Building powerful states, based on taxes, armies, laws, and so forth, became the focus of these elites. Many states, successful in their state-building efforts, enjoyed considerable longevity and impact on the people they ruled.

### Islamic Dynasties

The Mongol invasions and the Black Death left the Islamic world in tatters. Great centers of Islamic learning and civilization were destroyed. The Mongols, however, failed to establish a long-lasting regime in their place. Unwilling to share power with local, conquered peoples, the Persian Il-khans had no base on which to build a more permanent system of government. Instead, they relied on brute force and intimidation to maintain their positions of power. When factionalism broke out among the Mongol overlords, their power fell apart. Within the power vacuum of southwestern Asia, new contenders began to rise. Beginning small, the Ottomans and Safavids gradually attracted followers and built power.

As these post-Mongol states expanded, the borders of Islam began to extend outward. What had existed primarily as an

Arabic-speaking culture with some Turks and Persians, soon spread to new vistas in which Turkish and Persian speakers rose as the majority. With the sixteenth century, three emerging Islamic empires began to dominate the Islamic world: the Ottomans in Anatolia (and around the Mediterranean), the Safavids in Persia, and the Mughals in India.

## THE RISE OF THE OTTOMAN EMPIRE

The Turkish Ottomans rose to power under the leadership of Osman. Beginning as Islamic warrior bands, they defeated rival bands and conducted a holy war against Christian Byzantines. Based in Bursa, the Ottomans avoided the primary failure of the Mongols by establishing a system of rule that attracted and included educated urbanites. At the top of the system sat a sultan who oversaw both military and civilian bureaucracies. By the mid-sixteenth century, the Ottomans had expanded into the Balkans as the most powerful force in the Middle East.

*The Tools of Empire Building*   Promises to new subjects fueled military expansion, which provided spoils for more expansion and rewards for followers. By sharing wealth and power, the Ottomans turned conquered peoples into loyal subjects. In 1453, only half a century after roaming as a nomadic tribe, the Ottomans conquered Constantinople and renamed it Istanbul. Suleiman the Magnificent continued the conquests. More than just a military man, he supported the arts and headed a government known for just and efficient rule. Istanbul had become the primary link between Europe and the Islamic world and the Ottomans reaped rewards in trade and status. Ottoman power also employed religion. Sultans combined features of the warrior with those of Islamic believers.

*The Conquest of Constantinople*   Military successes, such as the defeat of Constantinople, paved the way for the Ottomans' spectacular rise to power but it was their willingness to share that power that allowed them to keep their empire. While many lamented the fall of the Byzantine capital, fleeing refugees helped revive Europe's interest in the classical world of Greece and Rome. Meanwhile, the Ottomans seized control of Europe's access to the Indian Ocean trade.

*Istanbul and the Topkapi Palace*   Defending and promoting Islam, the Ottomans built mosques and schools, kept the peace, and protected Muslims from Christians and other rivals. The city of Istanbul and "the Magnificent" leader Suleiman reflected Islam's greatness. Rebuilding after the conquest, the Ottomans constructed palaces, mosques, walls, public buildings, bazaars, baths, and inns. Muslims and non-Muslims alike were invited to Istanbul, which eventually grew to a population of 400,000—the largest city outside China. From Topkapi Palace, the sultan governed via a large bureaucracy headed by the grand vizier. Topkapi also housed the sultan's harem of 12,000 or so women, ranging from slave girls to favorite consorts.

*Diversity and Control in the Ottoman Empire*   Reaching into Europe and North Africa, Ottoman streets hosted numerous languages, although Ottoman Turkish was the official language of governing. Regions were allowed significant autonomy. As long as they paid taxes and provided soldiers, local authorities governed themselves. This decentralized approach threatened Ottoman control, however, particularly as local leaders short-changed Istanbul. Thus, center-appointed administrators and janissaries, soldiers loyal to the sultan, were placed throughout the empire. Conscripted from Christian villages and trained as Islamic warriors, the janissaries became an elite corps of military and administrative leaders, loyal to the sultan only. Balancing local rule with central control, the Ottomans proved very successful at holding the crossroads between Europe and Asia.

## THE EMERGENCE OF THE SAFAVID EMPIRE IN IRAN

In Persia (modern Iran) the Safavid empire rose from the smoldering ruins of Mongol conquests. Here, Mongol rule had been particularly destructive and had offended local Muslims by using Jews and Christians as the area's new elite administrators. When Mongol rule crumbled, the area broke into chaos, with warrior chieftains fighting for influence and religious movements seeking followers. Safi al-Din, head of a religious brotherhood, managed to gain warrior and religious support.

As the Persian state rose, his successors, such as Shah Ismail, began to champion Shiism, killing those opposed to it and making it the state religion. The Safavids also claimed that God had given them divine right to rule. Ismail pronounced himself the first shah of the Safavid Empire. The Safavids did not tolerate diversity, insisting that all conform to the standards of the theocratic regime. As a result, they were never as successful in expanding as the Ottomans.

## THE DELHI SULTANATE AND EARLY MUGHAL EMPIRE

In 1206, the Delhi Sultanate rose in India. By the time the Mongols reached India in 1303, the Delhi Sultanate was strong enough to meet the Mongols with a powerful military force that drove them back (one of the few examples of Mongol failure). The sultanate embarked on campaigns of conquest for glory and resources, both to help support the large military and to aid further expansion of the empire.

Near the end of the fourteenth century, however, declining revenues and rising expenditures cut into the military budget. This, plus feuds within the military, ensured that the next great wave of invaders could not be turned back. Sweeping down from Central Asia, Timur wreaked havoc on Delhi itself before leaving with artisans and plunder. Religious movements then challenged the weakened Delhi authority, causing large regions like Bengal to break away. Other regional movements defied Delhi authority, and northern India broke into a variety of polities all competing for power. To gain advantage, the governor of Punjab asked Central Asian Turks from Afghanistan to help him against his rivals. Babur (the "Tiger") accepted the invitation, but then destroyed the Delhi Sultanate before proclaiming himself emperor of a new dynasty: the Mughal Dynasty.

The three Islamic dynasties all based their power on strong militaries, religious backing, and extensive bureaucracies. Since all three were expansive, they competed with each other. Nevertheless, Islam also gave them common ground, as did the exchange of goods and ideas.

## Western Christendom

In 1300, most of Europe's population of some 80 million still lived in small communities in the countryside. Urbanization, however, was increasing. Universities helped to spread knowledge, and inventions, such as the clock, began to appear. With the fourteenth century, however, these positive developments gave way to disaster. Cooling temperatures, exhausted soils, and heavy taxation crushed the peasantry, leading to failed harvests and famine that killed millions. Weakened by hunger, Europe's population was then set upon by the Black Death. People avoided each other. Crowded cities were decimated. Between 25 and 50 percent of Europe's total population died within five years. Outbreaks continued to the end of the century. Three centuries passed before the population recovered to preplague numbers.

REACTIONS, REVOLTS, AND RELIGION IN EUROPE

The disease greatly impacted all aspects of European life. The church, in particular, struggled. Many people turned to pleasure-seeking before they died. Others turned to extreme spirituality. For many, rational Christianity could not account for the losses to the plague. Others struggled with the loss of clerics, the representatives of church authority, many of whom died or simply fled. As religious leaders moved to reestablish their authority, some challenged the church, prompting church-led inquisitions that persecuted heretics, Jews, witches, and others. Raising money for its campaigns and other ventures, church leaders turned to selling indulgences, a practice that prompted the Protestant Reformation. Popular dissatisfaction also grew with the feudal system. Peasant rebellions broke out, protesting both the failure of lords to defend them from marauders and the imposition of feudal restrictions. French peasants rose up and killed lords and high clergy. In England, rioting peasants were ruthlessly crushed.

STATE-BUILDING AND ECONOMIC RECOVERY IN EUROPE

Leaders tried to reconstruct a stable society but never achieved the successes of Asia. No common language unified the political realms of Europe. In France, several different languages

thrived. Similarly, few models of centralized government inspired emulation. Rulers of local regions thus began to rise. Like dynasts elsewhere, they claimed divine legitimacy by performing sacred rituals and demanding that priests teach obedience to the king. They used marital alliances with other kings to gain support. Kings sponsored an official language for their state that all administrators were required to know. Military force was also employed as nobles and peasants alike resisted the court's efforts to tax or control them. Kings also instituted strict social hierarchies that extended from themselves, at the top, down through the nobles and clergy, learned lawyers, great merchants, artisans, and peasants, at the bottom. Family life reflected these hierarchies, with fathers governing mothers and children.

These efforts gave some control to the king, but people continued to rebel and organize themselves in defiance of the king's laws. Despite their efforts, European kings failed to approach anywhere near the success of the Asian rulers. Europe's communities were still very small and fragmented.

*Portugal* Under the House of Aviz, the Portuguese began to consolidate power. Promoting trade and religious contention against the Muslim threat, the crown built unity and pitched the country into a search for a direct sea route to Asia. Pressing into the Atlantic and down the coast of Africa, and attacking Muslim strongholds that threatened the way, Portuguese seamen gradually worked south. The crown won support of the nobles by granting them Atlantic islands like the Canaries on which sugar could be grown for profit. Threatened by outside rivals, the people of Portugal pulled together and eventually succeeded in sending a ship (under Bartholomew Diaz) around the tip of Africa. This and other successes helped Portugal to remain united in the chaotic period after the Black Death.

*Spain* Spain followed suit, but struggled with fragmentation even more than Portugal. In Spain, noble houses quarreled incessantly until marital alliances began to unite various regions in Spain. Unity was acheived by the marriage of Isabella of Castile and Ferdinand of Aragon in 1469. This union brought Spain's wealthiest province together with that hosting the country's most ambitious traders. The royal family also married children into other reigning families, strengthening Spanish rule.The crown then began to unite other regional lords, attack heretics via Inquisitions, and reclaim lost lands from Muslims, culminating in the conquest of Granada in 1492. Muslims that did not flee faced severe repression. The Spanish crown's campaigns and the costs they incurred, meanwhile, prompted support for Christopher Columbus's venture to the west, prompting Spain's attention to shift toward the Atlantic.

*France, and England* France and England spent most of the fourteenth and fifteenth centuries at war with each other. After finally ousting the English from the continent, France sought to rebuild power. Marriage alliances helped, although the French nobles in the various regions remained quite powerful for the next two centuries. After warring with France, civil war divided England before the Tudors took control. Even as kings rose to take power, they first emerged as merely the greatest of the nobles and could be challenged by members of the noble class. Nobles advised the king, governed their territories with autonomy, and pursued their own interests. Centralization, in short, still had a long way to go.

## EUROPEAN IDENTITY AND THE RENAISSANCE

Rising stability after the problems of the fourteenth century contributed to a cultural flowering in Europe. The Renaissance represents the expansion of knowledge and a renewed interest in the ancient culture of the Greeks and Romans, which had been largely ignored as "pagan" before the Renaissance. Scholars showed new interest in ancient societies for insights into geography, arts, philosophy, medicine, and natural history. Moving beyond sacred, church-dominated theology, Renaissance thinkers began studying the secular humanities and using their discoveries to judge Europe's current conditions.

Printing spread ideals of wealth, knowledge, and cultivation. Kings began to follow these ideals by purchasing paintings and sculpture, patronizing artists, and supporting scholars. Merchants followed suit, and even the church began to support the new movement in limited ways. Renaissance scholars and artists used their new influence to advocate political changes modeled on political structures of the ancient Greeks. Other thinkers defended the church and the secular authorities. In Florence, a political movement featuring commercial interests and Renaissance values, like patriotism, liberty, and civic virtue, emerged as a new model for government. Machiavelli challenged these ideas, claiming that virtue meant nothing without successful statecraft to back it up.

Rivalries between Renaissance thinkers, commercial interests, and political authorities ensured that no consensus or unifying rule could emerge. Nevertheless, the ideals of good government, freedom of thought, civilization, and stability that eventually came to characterize parts of Europe and delineated it from the "barbarism" of the rest of the world.

## Ming China

The Mongols also devastated China. Ironically, the Black Death brought by the Mongols contributed to their demise as rulers of China. Despite tremendous development, productivity could not keep up with population growth. Already weakened by food shortages, Chinese fell to the Black Death in horrifying numbers. In Hebei province as much as 90 percent of the population succumbed. The Mongol leaders of China's Yuan dynasty could not cope. Religious movements, sounding the end of the world, sprang up to challenge the government. Zhu Yuanzhang, a peasant of very humble origin, rose to take charge of the Red Turbans before moving to challenge Mongol rule in China.

## CENTRALIZATION UNDER THE MING

Zhu took the southern city of Nanjing as his new capital, founded the Ming ("brilliant") dynasty, declared himself its first emperor (the Hongwu emperor), and moved to drive the Mongols from northern China. After defeating rival rebel leaders, Zhu moved to reconstruct the remnants of China's shattered society. He began by rebuilding Nanjing and fortifying its massive walls. (The third emperor, Yongle, moved the capital to Beijing and built the enormous Forbidden City as a majestic symbol of the emperor's power.) The Hongwu emperor initially sent his sons to defend the northern border against renewed Mongol attacks. When they failed to heed his commands, he reduced their power and built a huge bureaucracy selected from exam-degree holders. He eliminated the position of prime minister, chief post in the bureaucracy, so he could govern it himself. He took prime interest in direct administration, determining salaries, appointing officials, forming the examination system—all to augment his own power. Thus, the Ming established the world's most rational but also most centralized system: one that sought the classification of people into hierarchies even down to the village level.

## RELIGION UNDER THE MING

The Hongwu Emperor also took control of Chinese religion as a means of legitimizing his rule. Cults and ritual were classified and made to revolve around the emperor's central role as the performer of sacrifices and mediator between the human realm and supernatural realm. In spite of the powerful role of government in religious life, local Buddhist and Daoist cults maintained remarkable independence and refused to be subordinated to the state hierarchy. Many local administrators dared not interfere with local religious organizations lest local ire be provoked.

## MING RULERSHIP

The Ming's extensive bureaucracy allowed the dynasty to establish a stable society, remarkable for its sheer size. To gain allegiance and taxes from small communities far from the emperor's throne, the emperor employed a system of local leaders, selected from among the local residents. These local leaders often had blood ties to the various families in their small communities and provided local peoples some autonomy from government officials like the magistrate. Nevertheless, sometimes autonomy went too far. When he felt his authority was threatened, the Hongwu Emperor killed some 100,000 people, including military men, scholars, and even members of his own bureaucracy. With so much power in the hands of the emperor, Ming China suffered from insufficient government. Given China's immense population, one man could not do it all. The system did, however, allow the Ming to remain powerful for a very long time.

TRADE UNDER THE MING

As the Ming stabilized conditions in China, trade began to rebound, including long-distance trade. Chinese goods such as silks and porcelains were sought the world over, prompting merchants to converge on Chinese ports. As trade in Southeast Asia expanded and accelerated Indian Ocean trade, China's southern ports became major trading hubs. Fearful that expanding trade would empower a rising merchant class and bring foreign contact that might undermine his rule, the Hongwu Emperor banned private trade. After his death, however, trade exploded as merchants and officials alike defied the ban to engage in the lucrative practice.

The Ming court itself engaged in official maritime ventures. To head these enormous missions to the seas, the Yongle Emperor sent a trusted eunuch named Zheng He. The voyages did not seek conquest or economic gain, but aimed to signal China's greatness to the known world and establish tributary relations with "lesser peoples" to the south. Communities willing to accept Chinese dominance were given permission to trade with China. Those that did not faced attack from Chinese armies. Rulers establishing tributary ties were expected to pay tribute to the Chinese emperor, but generally received gifts worth much more than their own tribute in return.

In 1433, the voyages suddenly ceased. Reviving Mongol threats led to official criticism for the expensive voyages to the southern seas. Thus official journeys ended, leaving the seas to intrepid private Chinese traders willing to defy the imperial ban. Stimulated by trade, maritime networks expanded. Southeast Asian ships grew to enormous size, as much as 1,000 tons. Muslims extended their reach while Japanese pirates began plundering the sea lanes. Europeans even began to arrive, but in small ships and small numbers relative to the vast numbers of ships and tons of goods being moved by Asian traders.

## QUESTIONS FOR CLASS DISCUSSION

1. Besides trade, what other forms of contact between peoples might have contributed to the spread of the bubonic plague through all of Afro-Eurasia?

2. Why did the early Ming send out maritime voyages? What was the motivating factor?

3. Some cultures implemented tolerant policy. Others did not. What might the advantages be of flexible tolerance and under what conditions might it work best?

4. How did the problems of Europe stimulate trade? Why did the Chinese emperor not show the same interest as the European kings?

5. How did Islamic sultans and Chinese emperors augment their power? Can any comparisons be drawn between the systems founded by each? Any differences?

## MULTIPLE-CHOICE QUESTIONS

1. Based on our understanding today, which of the following did *not* contribute to the spread of the Black Plague?
   a. fleas
   b. astrological changes
   c. rats
   d. ships
   e. trade routes

2. The epidemic associated with the Black Plague impacted history in all *except* which of the following ways?
   a. It killed tens of millions in China.
   b. It destroyed agriculture and led to famine by destroying farmers.
   c. It drained cities as people sought food and security in the countryside.
   d. It contributed to a growing sense of desolation among survivors.
   e. It strengthened the power of church and state wherever it hit.

3. Which of the following was *not* a means by which monarchs strengthened their rule during the fourteenth century?
   a. They earned legitimacy by claiming divine sanction.
   b. They crushed all influence and power of the church.
   c. They built up armies.
   d. They established laws and punishments.
   e. They established rules of succession to keep their lineage in power.

4. How did the Mongol invasions contribute to the rise of the Ottomans and Safavids?
   a. The Mongols founded these two long-lasting empires.
   b. The Mongols introduced government to these two empires.
   c. The Mongols destroyed these two empires.
   d. The Mongols destroyed old states, leaving a vacuum that the two empires could then fill.
   e. The Mongols traded with the two empires.

5. The Mongols
   a. failed to establish enduring dynasties in the Islamic territories they conquered.
   b. failed to conquer Baghdad.
   c. failed against powerful Islamic armies.
   d. succeeded at unifying the people they defeated.
   e. succeeded at winning the hearts of peasants everywhere they went.

6. Ottoman power rested on all of the following *except*
   a. military might.
   b. religious authority.
   c. great leadership.
   d. flexibility and tolerance in politics.
   e. harsh repression of all peoples under their rule.

7. The position of sultan combined all of the following social functions *except* that of
    a. superstar athlete.
    b. religious leader.
    c. military commander.
    d. wealthy patron of arts.
    e. defender of the faith.

8. The Safavid Empire persecuted those who did not follow
    a. Shiism.
    b. Christianity.
    c. Sunnism.
    d. Judaism.
    e. Paganism.

9. After the Delhi Sultanate collapsed in India, it was replaced by the
    a. Ottoman Empire.
    b. Byzantine Empire.
    c. Safavid Empire.
    d. Mongol Empire.
    e. Mughal Empire.

10. How did the Black Death impact the church's influence in Europe?
    a. It greatly augmented the status of clergy in Europe.
    b. It led to increased donations for the church.
    c. It contributed to the rapid spread of Christianity among non-Christian peoples in Europe.
    d. Among some believers, it stimulated hostility and resentment against the church.
    e. It caused the church to collapse.

11. The Renaissance was characterized by all of the following *except*
    a. rising interest in Roman and Greek antiquity.
    b. increased attention to the arts.
    c. new visions and models of government.
    d. heightened emphasis on education.
    e. broadening recognition that humans are worthless.

12. In Europe the printing press
    a. was completely ignored.
    b. gave voice to political views different from those of the king.
    c. proved extremely unpopular among the lower classes.
    d. was unknown until about 1820.
    e. remained within the control of the church and king.

13. The Ming dynasty emperors based their power on all of the following *except*
    a. the Forbidden City.
    b. an extensive bureaucracy selected by an examination.
    c. an elite class of warriors called the janissaries.
    d. an elaborate protocol of rites and ceremonies.
    e. terror.

14. The Chinese armada headed by Zheng He during the Ming dynasty was
    a. small and insignificant.
    b. limited to shallow coastal waters around China.
    c. generally defeated by its enemies.
    d. proved by its distant travels to be the world's greatest at the time.
    e. small—it had fewer ships than Columbus did when he discovered the New World.

15. The Ming court generally felt that international trade was
    a. so important that it received special government protection.
    b. so important that merchants were given the highest status in the land.
    c. disruptive enough to ban it, but not so much to enforce the ban.
    d. unworthy of government attention.
    e. so dangerous that it was repressed at all costs.

## MAP EXERCISE

Looking at a map of the globe, identify the source of the Black Death and trace courses it may have followed to get to Europe. Also, identify regions where massive outbreaks of disease were likely to have occurred (i.e., densely populated areas like big cities on well-used trade routes).

## KEYWORDS

| | |
|---|---|
| bubonic plague | shah |
| Black Death | Bhakti Hinduism |
| mandate of heaven | Yuan Mongols |
| Il-khanate | Red Turbans |
| Sunni Islam | Ming dynasty |
| Topkapi Palace | Forbidden City |
| sultan | examination system |
| harem | jong |
| *devshirme* | Beghards |
| janissaries | Flagellants |
| viziers | Jacquerie |
| Sufi brotherhoods | scrofula |
| Shiism | Renaissance |

## ANSWERS TO MULTIPLE-CHOICE QUESTIONS

| | | |
|---|---|---|
| 1. b | 6. e | 11. e |
| 2. e | 7. a | 12. b |
| 3. b | 8. a | 13. c |
| 4. d | 9. e | 14. d |
| 5. a | 10. d | 15. c |

## CHAPTER 12

# Contact, Commerce, and Colonization, 1450s–1600

## CHAPTER OBJECTIVES

- To explain the growth of contact between different parts of the globe in an age of exploration, mercantile trade, and colonization
- To identify the impact of the discovery of the New World
- To maintain that the Islamic and East Asian empires remained dominant, even as European ties to Asia began to strengthen

## CHAPTER OUTLINE, CHRONOLOGY, AND SUMMARY

Magellan's circumnavigation of the world produced the first world travelers: those who had visited all parts of the globe, including the Americas. The discovery of a "New World" profoundly changed economic and political relationships across the globe as Europeans became stronger competitors within international trading networks. The great Asian empires—Ming, Ottoman, and Mughal—continued to enjoy supremacy, but the balance of military and economic might began to tip in favor of the Europeans.

### The Old Trade and the New

In the fifteenth century, European merchants revived shattered trading networks and built new ones—particularly maritime networks in the Indian Ocean and the China Sea. In search of vast profits, European merchants explored the coast of Africa and eventually found a direct passage to Asia. At the same time, Columbus found sponsorship to try a westward route and ran into the Americas. Europeans sought converts and wealth in Asia. What they learned, however, was just how far behind Asia Europe really was.

THE REVIVAL OF THE CHINESE ECONOMY

Commercial activity during the Ming dynasty soared, even after the capital moved north to Beijing. A rising population, which doubled during the Ming, meant larger markets, thus stimulating economic production. Rebuilding the Grand Canal provided a link between northern and southern China and thus stimulated the growth of commercial centers along its banks. Cities became huge. Nanjing had over one million people, while Canton and Foshan alone housed more people than all the city dwellers of Europe combined.

By the fifteenth century, merchant activity was generally tolerated, allowing artisans to produce vast quantities of silks and porcelains. Chinese at court, kept most (and the best) of China's goods, but a healthy percentage of the goods made it into interregional trading networks where they were exchanged for silver. China's burgeoning economy lacked only specie, ensuring that China's trading partners had to supply it if they wanted to get Chinese goods. Japan supplied much of China's silver, but that trade was later eclipsed when huge stores of American silver were discovered.

REVIVAL OF INDIAN OCEAN TRADE

Trade in the Indian Ocean also rose as Muslim merchants sailed everywhere from Africa to Southeast Asia in search of profits. In the center sat the Indian subcontinent, with its vast cities, exotic goods, and productive manufacturing centers. Indian traders, although also confronted with China's demands for silver, did not find themselves under the thumb of any single political authority. They thus enjoyed more flexibility in long-distance trade than their Chinese counterparts. The most significant trading port in the Indian Ocean was Melaka, which bridged trade between the Indian Ocean and the South China Sea. As an entrepot of world trade, Melaka possessed an extraordinarily diverse community, eventually joined by Western Europeans.

OVERLAND COMMERCE AND OTTOMAN EXPANSION

Overland trading did not cease with rising marine trade but, in fact, expanded along some routes. A northern route linked the Baltic Sea and northern China while a southern route brought Chinese and Indian goods through Ottoman lands into Europe. On the southern route, Aleppo in Syria dominated silk trade for all the Middle East. There, merchants held special status and were celebrated in literature for their courage and cunning in organizing enormous caravans.

Ottoman authorities showed particular interest in trade and gained considerably from it through taxes. Refreshment stations were built to accommodate merchants, their animals, and wares. Military stations protected trade from Bedouin raiders, who plundered both caravans and refreshment stations. Taxes on trade gave the Ottomans revenues for building military might and helped expansion westward across northern Africa into the Balkans. By the middle of the fifteenth century, the Ottomans were able to take Constantinople and rename it Istanbul.

Christendom was shocked. Ottoman expansion had taken a bastion of Christianity, threatened Venice, and controlled the Mediterranean. The spread of Ottoman control worried European merchants, who feared that they would be excluded from Asian markets just as global trade was expanding. Islamic traders were fierce rivals. European naval attacks against Ottoman control of the Mediterranean, however, failed. Europe would have to find another way to access Asia.

## European Exploration and Expansion

With the Ottomans blocking land routes to Asia, Europeans began searching for other routes. Russians pressed east across Siberia. Others sailed south around Africa or west where they accidentally encountered the Americas.

THE PORTUGUESE IN AFRICA AND ASIA

The lure of African gold and silver provided additional inspiration to Portuguese seeking to find a route around Africa. To carry them to riches, the Portuguese constructed hybrid ships that combined technology of the Greeks and Arabs. Sailing their caravels, Portuguese learned how to tack into the wind, while the compass, astrolabe, and newer maps gave direction. Military advances in gunpowder ensured they could compete in a hostile environment. Conquering their own fears of the unknown and misinformation about what lay beyond, the Portuguese eventually rounded Africa.

Before getting to Asia, however, the Portuguese learned to profit from Africa. On the coast, they built small trading ports. On islands off the African coast, they established sugar plantations worked by African slaves—the first examples of slave-powered plantations. Many slaves were sent to Portugal as domestic servants.

Portuguese traders sought profit, not colonies. The first to reach Asia was Vasco da Gama. On reaching Africa's eastern coast, he quickly acquired a Muslim pilot to guide his ship to India. There he overcame local resistance, including his own kidnapping, loaded his ships with goods, and sailed back to Lisbon, arriving in 1499. Subsequent voyages proved the Portuguese to be fierce competitors as they burned rival ships and killed their sailors. With the way charted, the Portuguese began establishing a presence at major Indian Ocean ports, including Aden, Hormuz, and Melaka. Using threats of violence and the *cartaz* (pass) system, Portugal's traders controlled portions of the Indian Ocean trade, allowing the trade of Asian goods via Portuguese ports to overshadow that of Italian ports—formerly Europe's most important.

Sixteenth-century Lisbon oversaw the rise of a trading and plantation empire based on small colonies (African islands) and naval control of the trading lanes. Larger territorial acquisitions would not come, however, until the discovery of the Americas.

## The Atlantic World

Europe's accidental discovery of America opened a new epoch in history but it was European diseases, not guns, which had the greatest impact. Declining Amerindian populations opened the way for Europeans but cut short the potential labor force, thus spawning demand for African slaves in America as plantations developed and gold and silver were mined. This Atlantic trade gave Europeans an edge: complete control of a lucrative trade unavailable to anyone else. Spain and Portugal opened the network to Asia and America, but soon found other European powers scrambling for a share, with great consequence.

WESTWARD VOYAGES OF COLUMBUS

Columbus changed history but was a product of his times. His desire to spread Christianity and earn money typified the goals of most Europeans and led to the creation of the Atlantic system. Soon others made the journey west and discovered the significance of Columbus's efforts.

## FIRST ENCOUNTERS

Claiming the new land, Columbus noted that the natives cut themselves on the sharp edges of his sword, symbolizing the dramatic technological disparities between the two peoples. Columbus wrote of their childlike innocence, while others were described as savages—the two primary stereotypes Europeans created about Amerindians. Amerindians viewed the Europeans with curiosity, fear, and loathing. As time progressed, however, it was generally acknowledged that the Europeans had come as conquerors.

## FIRST CONQUESTS

Reports of gold brought many more Spaniards to the Americas. Amerindians were soon pressed into virtual slavery in the search for gold. The Spanish crown institutionalized the practice by granting the privilege of exploiting the labor of certain Indian communities. Local overlords thus grew rich while the natives suffered horribly, dying of disease, dislocation, and malnutrition in shocking numbers. Settlers argued over privilege. Meanwhile, angry at the poor treatment of the natives, Dominican friars sharply condemned the practice, thus dividing Europeans over the fate of the Amerindians. Nevertheless, exploitation continued.

## THE AZTEC EMPIRE AND THE SPANISH CONQUEST

Some Europeans moved on and discovered complex societies in Central America. The Aztec rulers governed about 25 million people, many of whom lived in large cities administered by an elaborate array of priests, military leaders, and government officials. These in turn were supported by a host of village elders united by marital arrangements with the families of other villages. Elite families in the capital did the same, creating a class of natural leaders. Priests helped maintain order and selected sacrifices necessary to keep the sun burning and rains falling.

By the end of the fifteenth century, military successes allowed the Aztecs to dominate Mesoamerica, earning plunder, tribute, and human sacrifices needed to sustain the god of the sun. Resenting their plight, non-Aztec tribes rebelled, particularly the Tláxcalans and Tarascans. By the time of Moctezuma II, the strain of military expenditures and division among political leaders began producing cracks in Aztec unity and control. Sightings of arriving Europeans only added further confusion. Moctezuma sent jewels and prized feathers to the Europeans, but made no effort to fortify his own people.

Cortés acquired translators and marched on Mesoamerica. Entering the Aztec capital of Tenochtitlán, he and his men marveled at its splendor before allying with Aztec rivals, the Tlaxcalans, and capturing Moctezuma. Two years later, conflict between Spanish and Aztecs led to a massive uprising in which Moctezuma was killed and hundreds of Spaniards were sacrificed to the Aztec sun god. Regrouping with Tlaxcalan allies, Cortés returned with cannon to destroy Aztec resistance. Disease, however, did much of the fighting for him. Upon their return, the Spaniards discovered the Aztec defenders dying from smallpox.

The war against the Aztecs taught the Europeans that Amerindian rivals had to be crushed quickly, before they realized the intruders weren't gods. It also illuminates the tremendous impact that disease could play.

## THE INCAS

In Incan lands, civil war and disease weakened the Incan regime even before European rivals arrived. Capturing the emperor, Pizarro's forces destroyed the Incas and opened the way for Spanish *encomiendas* to take over. Factionalism among the Spaniards, however, meant that war only continued before the Spanish crown intervened.

The collapse of the Aztecs and Incas meant Europeans had access to new wealth, new markets, and new frontiers.

## "THE COLOMBIAN EXCHANGE"

Europeans gained more than gold from the New World. Tomatoes, beans, cacao, peanuts and others items made their way to Europe as well, greatly transforming European diets. Amerindians got wheat, grapes, sugar, cattle, horses, and a transformation of the local flora and fauna as European plants and animals overwhelmed native species. Europeans and Africans also brought diseases that ravaged local populations. Smallpox epidemics were soon followed by measles and others, leading to the destruction of about 90 percent of the Amerindian population and leaving the New World wide open to European dominance.

## SPAIN'S TRIBUTARY EMPIRE

The Spaniards supplanted the Aztec and Incan hierarchies while leaving most of the administrative structure intact. This allowed them to rule without having to fully reconstruct a bureaucratic system. Villagers offered goods and services to the Spanish as they had done to their Aztec leaders. *Encomenderos* forced Indian laborers to work in mines, on plantations, or on public works for their own profit. Another change involved the rise of the mestizos, peoples of mixed Amerindian and Spanish blood, who came to dominate after severe shortages of European women led many European men to take native women. Most Spaniards lived in cities, either ports or great capitals built on the ruined cities of conquered peoples.

## SILVER

Discovering large quantities of specie in lands taken from the Aztecs and Incas, the Spanish shipped as much as possible to Spain. Within the first two decades after conquering the Aztecs, the Spanish transported more gold than all of Europe then possessed. After seizing Amerindian stores, the Spanish turned to mining silver from great deposits in Mexico and the Andes. These mines produced huge quantities of precious metal while also consuming countless lives of the Amerindians compelled to work in them. Filling European coffers, silver changed the balance of power in Europe and the balance of European trade in Asia—particularly with China and India.

## PORTUGAL'S NEW WORLD COLONY

The pope compelled Spain to share the New World with Portugal. While Brazil did not produce great mines, its vast tracts of extremely fertile land proved lucrative enough. Royal grants gave ambitious individuals great estates, which they administered from the safety of enclaves. Scattered tribes of reluctant and rebellious Amerindians could not produce sufficient labor pools to work the land, so the Portuguese turned to importing African slaves.

On their islands off the coast of Africa, Portuguese had already developed a model for sugar production. Soon the model appeared in Brazil and the Caribbean, making New World sugar production more lucrative than silver production. Most slaves were men working under extremely harsh conditions on the small plantations. So many slaves perished that the demand for new shipments from Africa remained high year after year.

## BEGINNINGS OF THE TRANSATLANTIC SLAVE TRADE

Transatlantic slaving arose to supply sugar plantations with labor. Insatiable demands for sugar meant an insatiable demand for slaves. By 1820, five times more Africans had journeyed to the New World than Europeans. The Portuguese initiated the trade but were soon joined by many other European powers. While the Islamic world actually took more African slaves than did the Europeans, they did so over a much longer period of time. Africans themselves had also long engaged in slave-trading. Nevertheless, European slaving reached stunning proportions. Few areas remained unaffected by European or Asian slave networks. To Africans engaged in the capture and sale of slaves to the Portuguese, the high price tag on individuals meant that it was more profitable to sell them than to keep them as agricultural workers, thus contributing to Africa's underdevelopment.

By the end of the sixteenth century, an Atlantic system had emerged based on African labor, American minerals and land, and European technology and military power. With time, this shift in wealth and people would disrupt the global balance of power.

## The Transformation of Europe

The opening of the Atlantic system may have empowered Europe, but it in no way united Europeans. Religious rivalries continued to tear at European integrity.

### THE HABSBURGS AND THE QUEST FOR UNIVERSAL EMPIRE IN EUROPE

The Habsburgs nearly created a unified European world. Enormous territorial holdings, strategic marriage alliances, and victorious campaigns, however, could not entirely overcome the difficulties of holding a vast empire together. Warfare from within and without, particularly in the Ottoman Empire, led to great instability and eventual breakup. With most of the specie and land of the New World controlled by the Holy Roman Empire or Spanish Habsburgs, French, English, and Dutch interests moved to get their share. Discovering no gold or trade route to Asia, they profited by pirating Spanish ships and ports. Some, like Sir Francis Drake, received commissions from their monarchs to plunder their Spanish rivals. Rivalry on the high seas climaxed in 1588 when England's Royal Navy destroyed the Spanish Armada in the English Channel, giving the English supremacy at sea.

### THE REFORMATION

Other divisions developed as well. The Protestant Reformation split church solidarity and forced monarchs to choose between either the Catholic or the Protestant cause. Martin Luther, following the footsteps of earlier "heretics," defied the Catholic Church and called for its reform (hence the "Reformation"). Denouncing corruption, he claimed that salvation came by faith of the individual and rested in biblical truths, not church authority. He also translated the Bible into German so common people could read it. As printing presses and ardent preachers spread his ideas, they met a receptive audience. Calvinism, Anglicanism, and other Protestant sects soon arose as well, thus offering some measure of religious diversity. Although equally committed in their opposition to the Catholic Church, rivalries between Protestants also kept them divided.

The Catholics responded with the Counter-Reformation, a move to assert Catholic "correctness" in doctrine as well as to clean out alleged corruption among its clergy. Catholics also began to emphasize individual spirituality and to more fervently engage in proselytizing efforts as represented by the Society of Jesus (or Jesuits). The Catholic Church continued to meet "heresy" with repression and attack but could not prevail against Protestant notions spread by printing presses.

## RELIGIOUS WARFARE IN EUROPE

Religious rivalries soon climaxed in warfare, greatly weakening the Spanish while strengthening the English, French, and Dutch. As Luther's ideas spread, monarchs and princes favored or opposed them, often offending commoners and precipitating uprisings. Both sides gathered armies, leading to the formation of huge militaries comprised of common people. Decades of war allowed first German princes and then the Dutch to break away from the dominance of Catholic Spain and bankrupted the Spanish Habsburgs. Seizing initiative, the Dutch and English expanded ties to Asia and the New World, thus precipitating trade wars.

Religious conflict also broke out within countries as Catholics and Protestants massacred each other in the name of God. In France, the Protestant king converted to Catholicism and ordered some toleration to stem the violence. With time, this commitment to religion translated into commitment for this or that nation. Rather than viewing themselves as members of Christendom, Europeans identified with their king and his nation, marking another set of rivalries dividing Europe into fiercely competitive states.

## Growth of Trade in Asia

While Europe struggled with religious warfare, Asian empires flourished.

### MUGHAL INDIA AND COMMERCE

Powerful and wealthy, Mughal India barely even noticed the European presence. The military might of Babur only increased under his grandson Akbar who also consolidated control through marital alliances and power-sharing with Hindu princes. Noting India's remarkable diversity, Akbar ruled with tolerance. While Europeans slaughtered each other over religious differences, Akbar's tolerant policies allowed different religions to coexist in peace.

Mughal India also grew fabulously wealthy through trade. Mughal treasuries filled, allowing more for military and luxury spending. In the latter, the Mughals were unsurpassed. Grand architecture and art, gold, silk brocades, pearls, carpets, perfumes, and so forth, decorated palaces and elite homes throughout the empire. In short, the grandeur and power of Mughal India still far surpassed that of Europe and kept Europeans on the outskirts of the empire.

Despite Portugal's efforts to monopolize European trade with Mughal India, other Europeans eventually came to be involved. Trade provided sufficient revenue so Mughal lead-

ers could shift taxes from kind to monetary payments, thus creating a more efficient and effective system and supplying the throne with more funds. Commercialization allowed the court to tax as much as one third of all rural produce. Balance between merchants and the court allowed the Mughals considerable stability.

### PROSPERITY IN MING CHINA

Similar developments could be found in China where the economy also expanded. Bans on foreign trade were ignored as Chinese goods were exchanged for silver. As in India, the availability of silver stimulated commercialization and the exchange of money instead of kind. With more money available, the Chinese could improve agriculture and develop industries like textiles. Prosperity stimulated population increases. The population of China reached 250 million or over one third of the world's total. China's huge cities continued to expand with even more palaces, temples, educational institutions, and other associations. European Jesuit missionaries seeing China's greatness firsthand marveled at the wealth and liveliness of the cities. Chinese women found multiple occupations as the economy and society diversified. The state, meanwhile, found it increasingly difficult to manage China's dynamic system.

### ASIAN RELATIONS WITH EUROPE

The Portuguese spearheaded Europe's presence in Asia. Arriving at Macao in 1557, they enjoyed Europe's only direct access to China. Noting Portuguese success, other Europeans followed. Spain reached Asia from the Pacific side, establishing themselves in the Philippines and using American silver to buy Chinese goods. High demand for silver in China and for Chinese goods in other areas allowed trade to expand and connect the entire globe.

The English, Dutch, and French were not to be left behind. In England, investors formed the English East India Company, which then moved to replace the Portuguese in the Arabian Sea and the Persian Gulf before moving on to India. Despite these new contacts with Asia, however, European influence still remained a distant second to that of the great Asian powers.

## QUESTIONS FOR CLASS DISCUSSION

1. Why did the Ottomans encourage trade? Other than the obvious economic advantages, what else might trade have offered the Ottoman regime?

2. What compelled the Europeans to search for an avenue to Asia? Why were monarchs in Europe willing to fund such voyages?

3. What about the Spanish conquistadors allowed them to so handily conquer the great Aztec and Incan empires? What element was the most important and why?

4. The New World gave Europeans access to remarkable new sources of revenue. Describe the various ways one could make a fortune in the Americas. Which of these various ways was "best" and why?

5. How did the Reformation change Europe politically and socially?

## MULTIPLE-CHOICE QUESTIONS

1. Before the discovery of opium, what was the primary commodity used by the Europeans to trade with the Chinese?
   a. woolen goods
   b. wooden goods
   c. wheat
   d. silver
   e. porcelain

2. Much of China's silver imports came from Japan and
   a. the New World.
   b. Russia.
   c. Mongolia.
   d. India.
   e. Africa.

3. Of the following, who were *not* primary traders in the Indian Ocean trade before the Portuguese made it to India?
   a. Chinese
   b. British
   c. Muslims
   d. Indians
   e. Southeast Asians

4. How did the Ottoman regime view trade?
   a. It actively encouraged and protected trade.
   b. It sought to restrict trade at all costs.
   c. It limited overland caravan trade and encouraged overseas trade.
   d. It moved to stimulate trade but restrict merchants.
   e. The Ottomans did not trade.

5. The Ottoman conquest of Constantinople spread panic among Europeans who
   a. feared the Ottomans would sever European ties to Asian markets.
   b. believed that the city would be burned.
   c. feared that the end of the world was coming.
   d. believed that the Ottomans would no longer trade with Europe.
   e. feared that diseases would spread to Europe.

6. Which of the following statements about Portuguese exploration is *not* true.
   a. Portuguese exploration gradually took them around the southern tip of Africa.
   b. Portuguese shipbuilders borrowed technology from Greeks and Arabs.
   c. The Portuguese built sugar plantations on islands they discovered in the Atlantic.
   d. The Portuguese relied on cannon power to help them get a toehold in Asia.
   e. The Portuguese abandoned the Asian trade when it proved too costly.

7. After encountering the New World, Columbus
   a. knew precisely that he had found something unknown to Europeans.
   b. thought he had found Asia but accidentally "discovered" something else.
   c. found what he had always dreamed of finding.
   d. realized that he had not actually found a route to Asia.
   e. had no idea where he was.

8. During the days of Columbus, most Europeans viewed the peoples of the Americas as either
   a. landowners or peasants.
   b. warriors or farmers.
   c. childlike innocents or savages.
   d. witch doctors or scientists.
   e. athletes or administrators.

9. Which of the following did *not* constitute a part of Aztec society?
   a. traders, farmers, warriors, and priests
   b. an elaborate system of temples and religious beliefs
   c. huge cities
   d. a powerful class of warriors
   e. horses and steel

10. All of the following helped Spanish conquistadors against the Aztecs *except*
    a. steel weapons, cannons, horses, and dogs.
    b. Spanish sorcerers.
    c. a young Indian noble woman later called Do-a Marina and Indian allies of the Spanish.
    d. Aztec belief that the Spaniards were gods.
    e. European diseases.

11. Which of the following "commodity" lists best describes the Atlantic trade of the seventeenth century?
    a. silver, sugar, and slaves
    b. silk, opium, and servants
    c. tobacco, porcelain, and mercenaries
    d. soldiers, ships, and tea
    e. cotton, silk, and hemp

12. In the sixteenth century, the Reformation led to
    a. increasing peace and stability in Europe.
    b. religious warfare between Protestants and Catholics.
    c. greater support for the church among all Christians.
    d. attacks on Christianity and beliefs in God.
    e. widespread disinterest in all religion.

13. Under Akbar, Mughal India represented one of the world's
    a. poorest empires.
    b. most repressive empires.
    c. wealthiest empires.
    d. most war-ridden empires.
    e. smallest empires.

14. In its dealings with European traders, the Ming dynasty government
    a. forced them to live in an enclave separated from China by a wall.
    b. welcomed them to the capital.
    c. offered special privileges to entice them to China.
    d. built for them special residences in the port cities.
    e. allowed them into China but taxed them heavily.

15. Europeans were attracted to Asia's
    a. potential for conquest and empire.
    b. wealth and the profits it offered merchants and kings alike.
    c. ancient world religions.
    d. great cities and touring opportunities.
    e. wise sages and powerful philosophical traditions.

## MAP EXERCISE

Looking at a map of the globe, track the flow of major global commodities like silver, tea, silk, and porcelain between Europe and China before the discovery of the Americas. Then, track the flow of trade involving slaves, sugar, and silver after the discovery of the Americas. How did Europe's position fare as a result of the change? Who might have lost out besides the Africans and Amerindians?

## KEYWORDS

| | |
|---|---|
| Grand Canal | Quetzalcoátl |
| the silver islands | ecological imperialism |
| caravans | mestizos |
| caravansarais | Reformation |
| Hagia Sophia | Protestantism |
| Granada | Catholicism |
| *conversos* | Counter-Reformation |
| caravel | St. Bartholomew's Day |
| carrack | Massacre |
| Gold Coast | Huguenot |
| Atlantic system | Treaty of Tordesillas |
| *encomiendas* | *Din-I-Ilahi* |
| *encomenderos* | *zamindars* |
| conquistador | Fatehpur Sikri |
| Tlaxcalans | Jesuit |
| Tarascans | |

## ANSWERS TO MULTIPLE-CHOICE QUESTIONS

| | | | |
|---|---|---|---|
| 1. | d | 9. | e |
| 2. | a | 10. | b |
| 3. | b | 11. | a |
| 4. | a | 12. | b |
| 5. | a | 13. | c |
| 6. | e | 14. | a |
| 7. | b | 15. | b |
| 8. | c | | |

# CHAPTER 13 | Worlds Entangled, 1600–1750

## CHAPTER OBJECTIVES

- To note the dramatic changes in Europe as a result of new wealth and increasing economic integration
- To illuminate difficulties faced by other cultures at the same time

## CHAPTER OUTLINE, CHRONOLOGY, AND SUMMARY

From 1600 to 1750, trade continued to expand, facilitating global trade networks that tied all areas of the globe together. Demands for silver, sugar, spices, silks, cotton, and porcelain drove trade so that products from each major global region could be found virtually everywhere else. Enthusiasm for investment opportunities stimulated growth (and risk), but it was silver that allowed economies to become commercialized and began to strengthen the hand of European trade. Europeans and Africans began moving into new places while Europeans expanded their colonial reach. Competition led to bitter conflicts, challenging the preeminence of Afro-Eurasia's great centralized empires.

### Increasing Economic Linkages and Social and Political Effects

Rising economic integration had far-reaching impact on rulers and common people alike. Shortages or surpluses of key goods greatly affected prices across the globe, which could affect fortunes. Tremendous fortunes, in turn, provided funding for larger armies and ambitious ventures, but they could also divide merchant interests from those of their monarchs. Some states became stronger because of trade (England, France,

Holland, Japan). Others became increasingly destabilized by it (the Mughals, the Ming, the Ottomans, the Savafids).

EXTRACTING WEALTH: MERCANTILISM

Gold and silver production in Spanish and Portuguese colonies stimulated other European powers to seek colonies of their own. Few found gold, but many found wealth in the New World's fertile lands by building plantations or harvesting furs. Sugar production, for example, soared. Viewing the world through mercantilist eyes, Europeans saw colonies strictly as sources of revenue. Wealth was then quickly translated into military power. Economics and politics became closely intertwined with one providing resources and the other defense.

### New Colonies in the Americas

HOLLAND'S TRADING COLONIES

The Dutch began as transporters of cargo for other nations, but eventually sought their own route to Asia via a "northern passage" around the north end of the Americas. Exploration by the Dutch East India Company provided information about the Hudson River and the Iroquois, but no passage. Interest dried up, but some settlers established themselves on the river and began engaging in trade with the Iroquois. Others profited by pirating Spanish shipping. Still others formed the Dutch West India Company and established a presence in the Caribbean, which ended in bankruptcy in 1674 after the company failed to seize control of Portuguese sugar production. Although they failed as colonists in the Americas, the Dutch did succeed as businessmen and transporters, carrying goods and underwriting ventures. Their greatest successes, however, were to be found in Asia.

FRANCE'S FUR-TRADING EMPIRE

French interest in a northern passage took them up the St. Lawrence River to the Great Lakes. There, French missionaries attempted to convert Amerindians to Catholicism while settlers interacted with them as fur traders. Beaver skins harvested by Amerindians and bought by the French cemented links between both groups and led to accommodative ties rarely found between Europeans and Amerindians. Marital relations between French and Amerindians gave rise to mixed-blood *métis,* who brokered between the two peoples.

ENGLAND'S LANDED EMPIRE

Dislike of the English cemented close alliances between the French and the Amerindians. Building farms, the English displaced Amerindians from the land, leading to friction and conflict. In New England, Puritan demands for land contributed to vicious wars in the 1630s and 1670s. Virginia witnessed much of the same, especially after tobacco began to produce great profits and the desire for land increased. With time, Europeans and Africans began to outnumber Amerindians, pushing the latter to the west as more and more land was taken over. Unlike the French, who intermingled and intermarried with the Amerindians, the English maintained their distance. Pushing Indians to the west, arriving Europeans and Africans began to transform the Atlantic seaboard.

THE PLANTATION COMPLEX IN THE CARIBBEAN

In the Caribbean, the sugar plantations based on slave labor dominated, even on English- and French-controlled islands. Given sugar's enormous profits, competition between the powers was fierce. The industry was lethal, however, requiring continuous supplies of new slaves to replace those who died. Plantation managers worked malnourished slaves to death in the disease-ridden tropics under horrifying living conditions. Slaves worked six days a week from dawn to dusk at backbreaking work, which accelerated during harvest time. Life expectancy on a plantation was three years. Some slaves resisted, occasionally through violence, to the point that governments had to negotiate or ban the slave trade. Slaves that could simply ran away to communities in the mountains or interior, where they congregated in huge numbers. Even more resisted in quieter ways. The English founded extremely lucrative sugar plantations on Jamaica, while the French seized half of Santo Domingo (present-day Haiti). With time Europeans became increasingly entrenched in the Americas and wealthier for the experience.

## The Slave Trade and Africa

More Africans arrived in the Americas than Europeans, greatly enriching the latter while decimating the African communities of the former.

CAPTURING AND SHIPPING SLAVES

Europeans got their slaves from ancient African slaving networks. Some slaves went north or east to Muslim or Hindu shippers, who took them to Indian Ocean ports. As the demand for slaves in the Americas rose, however, more and more slaves were sent to Africa's west coast. Some 12 million slaves survived to arrive in the New World; many millions more perished on the journey or even before departing Africa.

In the interior, most slaves were captured by Africans operating secret societies, such as Ekpe. Ekpe ensured that slave capturers fulfilled their quotas and built networks extending deep into inner Africa. Once captured, slaves were transported to slave ports along the African coast. Here, many died of hunger and disease, waiting until a ship's hold was filled. Once the ships set sail, diseases often spread, leading to mortality rates of 20 percent or so.

SLAVERY'S GENDER IMBALANCE

About two thirds of African slaves were men, disrupting sex ratios in Africa and the Americas. With reproduction among their slaves limited, slave owners in the Americas had to consistently depend on new arrivals to replenish the labor pool. In Africa, great plantations of female slaves became the norm. In some cases, such as Dahomy in West Africa, women asserted power because of their large numbers.

AFRICA'S NEW SLAVE-SUPPLYING POLITIES

The slave trade profoundly altered African development. African slavers and merchants who captured and sold slaves to European buyers profited greatly. For everyone else in Africa, the slave trade left terrible destruction. Regional leaders fought over control of the slave trade. Populations disappeared as men sporting firearms rounded up large numbers of people. Slaving tribes, enriched by the trade, bought more weapons and established their own plantations, served by enslaved women.

The Asante used locally acquired gold to purchase weapons and dominate their neighbors before establishing a centralized state comprising almost all of present-day Ghana. Borders emerged. Roads led out of the capital in all directions to bring slaves back for trading. Based on the savanna, the Oyo people and their king employed large cavalry forces to engage the forest peoples and capture whole villages. These tribes profited and gained goods from the outside, while other Africans suffered terribly. Port cities harbored most wealth while the interior became impoverished and stripped of its rural population.

## Asia in the Seventeenth and Eighteenth Centuries

In Asia, European influence remained marginal. Nevertheless, parts of Asia, as in India and Southeast Asia, gradually fell to European colonial control.

## THE DUTCH IN SOUTHEAST ASIA

Determined to monopolize the spice trade of Southeast Asia, the Dutch East India Company (VOC) adopted aggressive policies against rivals. The VOC raised huge sums of capital —ten times that of the English East India Company—and quickly began to deepen Dutch influence in Southeast Asia. Under Jan Pieterszoon Coen, the Dutch razed Jakarta and built a fortress as a base. Later, Coen's forces liquidated the population of the Banda nutmeg islands before moving on to other targets. By 1670, Dutch ruthlessness had given them control of the Melakan spice trade. The Dutch also engaged in less violent enterprises, transporting Asian goods in legitimate transactions to provide bullion needed in the China trade. The new Dutch presence greatly diminished the role of the old cosmopolitan trading hubs of the Southeast Asian trading network. Now European-controlled outposts became dominant.

## TRANSFORMATIONS IN ISLAM

The Islamic empires better resisted European trade incursions but did encounter internal disruptions.

*The Safavid Empire* Suffering from weak leadership, Safavid unity began to disintegrate, opening cracks in the regime. The empire eventually collapsed under the double blow of external invasion, occurring when Afghan warriors sacked the capital in 1722 and internal rebellion racked the government in 1773.

*The Ottoman Empire* Ottoman successes began to reverse after Suleiman when the Habsburgs stopped Ottoman expansion in the west. Reversals and population pressures prompted many to note that the empire was in decline. Poor leadership also hurt. Global economic integration and increased supplies of money made it easier for Europeans to illegally purchase Ottoman goods with silver and avoid paying taxes. Increasingly impoverished, sultans borrowing from merchants found it more difficult to restrict their illegal activities. Abundant silver but fewer goods meant inflation, which greatly pressured artisans and peasants, who rebelled in protest. Economics became hopelessly out of balance. Parts of the empire also began to show greater independence from Ottoman rule. When the sultan sent Mamluk military and administrative officers to help raise falling Egyptian tax revenues, the officers simply allied themselves with Egyptian merchants and elites and kept most fiscal revenues for themselves.

The "Koprulu reforms" did allow the Ottomans to briefly raise revenues and regain lost territorial possessions. Enthusiasm for greatness even inspired renewed attacks on Christendom and plans to take Vienna. The attack, however, failed and the Ottomans were forced to relinquish major European holdings.

*The Mughal Empire* While the Ottomans floundered, the Mughals flourished, controlling more of India than any prior empire. Akbar's successors continued to expand into the reaches of India and, by 1689, even controlled most of the south. Indian Ocean trade proved lucrative but was not pursued overseas. Mughal leaders remained content to tax land owners and let trade come to India—a simple decision given the eagerness of the Europeans. Trade increased wealth, led to the use of silver as the medium of exchange, and provided new crops for Indian peasants.

Commercial prosperity, however, also strengthened the hand of local and regional magnates seeking ways to build their own autonomy and challenge centralized Mughal rule. In the south, Marathas resistance consumed military resources and court finances. Eager to keep the south, Sultan Aurangzeb raised peasant taxes while also favoring Muslims over Hindus, thus creating hostility. Aurangzeb's death in 1707 was followed by a war of succession and outrageous taxation practices. Local elites moved to strengthen their own hands and assert independence, thus transforming centralized Mughal rule into a loose association of provincial states.

Economically, Mughal India thrived. New lands came into agrarian production while India's textile industry spread among the peasantry. Local leaders encouraged ties with Europeans and created Indian trading companies to manage trade with the outsiders. Others ran vast networks that combined trade and tax-farming.

## FROM MING TO QING IN CHINA

Growing wealth among China's local leaders weakened central control of the Ming as it did the Mughals in India. Still officially banned, overseas trade produced no revenues for the court but greatly enriched local merchants and smugglers.

*Administrative Problems* Weak emperors plagued the Ming. The Wanli Emperor refused to play his role as an administrator. Being an emperor was difficult, filled with responsibilities that could be monotonous and tiring. Ceremony and dignity bored Wanli who thus began to ignore his officials and duties.

*Economic Problems* As leadership declined, China's economy experienced rapid growth and concomitant problems. Attracted by rising opportunities, Japanese pirates plagued the coastal regions. Silver imports stimulated growth and increased revenues but hurt the peasantry, who suffered from inflation when too much silver was injected into China's domestic economy and who struggled under money-changer exactions when it came time to pay taxes. In protest, peasants rebelled. Disruptions in the flow of silver from outside China also injured the local economy.

*The Collapse of Ming Authority* As natural disasters led to crop failure and famine in northern China, peasant outrage increased. Government cutbacks alienated scholarly and military elites whose discontent combined with that of the peasants to create explosive rebellions. One, headed by Li Zicheng, conquered Beijing in 1644. To defeat the rebels, Ming generals invited their northern "barbarian" enemies into China. The Manchus naturally accepted the invitation, but then refused to leave when their task of destroying Li Zicheng's army was complete.

*The Qing Dynasty Asserts Control*  Noting their minority status, the Manchus moved cautiously to consolidate power. They flexibly implemented policies that the Chinese could accept. Ever adapting, these leaders of the Qing dynasty, promoted Confucian ideals and patriarchal values, reformulated traditional social hierarchies, and promoted the family. Outer regions, with their own religious majorities, received their own administrative systems based on local mores. To deepen Qing authority, marriages between Manchu and Han were forbidden, Han officials had to wear Manchu dress, and Han Chinese were required to shave their foreheads and grow a long queue in traditional Manchu fashion, at the risk of losing their heads if they did not comply. As arbiters of public morality, the Qing placed bans on certain activities, but then struggled to enforce them.

*Expansion and Trade under the Qing*  Economic activity thrived in the eighteenth century. Expansion and tributary relations greatly extended Chinese influence. Merchants fostered trade in Southeast Asia or monopolized European trade by purchasing special government licenses. Quick to keep Europeans in their place, the Qing established the "Canton system" for Europeans exclusively, which prevented them from freely coming into China and kept them under close scrutiny. The most important trade, however, took place within China, largely because of its sheer size and partly because it remained unencumbered by government taxes or oversight. In short, China remained vastly wealthy and stable, despite the dynastic transition of the seventeenth century.

TOKUGAWA JAPAN

Despite rising external trading pressures, the Japanese managed to unify under the Tokugawa Shogunate. They also managed to control the foreigners and largely avoid western incursion.

*Unification of Japan*  Under the leadership of autonomous warlords or *daimyo* Japanese warrior elites called *samurai* struggled for influence and land, dividing the country's political authority into smaller domains. Despite the fragmentation and a laughably weak court, however, a centralized system emerged. Hideyoshi started the process, but it fell to the house of Tokugawa to complete the task.

Defeating rival daimyo, Tokugawa Ieyasu assumed the title of *shogun*, Japan's top military position, before constructing a new centralized system. He established clear rules of succession, moved the capital to Edo (his base, now called Tokyo), converted samurai from warriors to administrators, and secured adequate resources for his regime. An end of warfare coupled with prosperity tripled the population between 1550 and 1700.

*Foreign Affairs and Foreigners*  By 1600, Europeans had established considerable presence in Japan as traders and missionaries, but their constant bickering and rivalry disrupted stability. To stem foreign influence, Japanese authorities banned Christianity, leading to violent suppressions and the expulsion of foreign missionaries. Traders, who generally favored Tokugawa rivals in the west, were also restricted; only the Dutch could trade with Japan and only under strict supervision at one port. Thus, while Asian trade continued, European traders were tightly controlled. Russian interest in the north compelled the Tokugawa to take over Ezo (Hokkaido) as a barrier to Russian encroachments, thus providing the Japanese with more territory and a stronger sense of identity.

## Transformations of Europe

Between 1600 and 1750, religion, commerce, and warfare all helped transform Europe and changed the nature of political authority.

EXPANSION AND DYNASTIC CHANGE IN RUSSIA

Expanding rapidly through Siberia to the east, Muscovy (or later Russia) eventually became the world's largest state but destroyed steppe nomadic peoples in the process. This expansion also meant population increased from 6 million in 1550 to 20 million in 1700. For Ivan III, expansion meant security from steppe nomad incursions. Adding marital ties to the last Byzantine emperor also allowed him to claim Russian succession to the Orthodox Church, which had lost its base with the fall of Constantinople. Later monarchs claimed the title of tsar and continued to push armies or follow fur-traders through Siberia, establishing control over a wide range of languages and cultures.

Succession problems prompted Russian elites to support the Romanovs as Russia's new leaders. The Romanovs perfected a centralized system in which the tsar maintained absolute power over virtually everything and everyone, including the nobles. Legally bound to the land and their lords as serfs, peasants lived in primitive communal arrangements. Sufficient stability allowed Peter the Great and successors like Catherine the Great to continue expansion eastward and westward toward the Baltic Sea. Peter built a new capital—St. Petersburg—and signed a treaty with the Chinese.

Migrations of Slavs into Siberia soon shifted the balance between Russians and indigenous peoples. Serfs migrated to escape repressive lords. Heretics and other political prisoners were banished there. Limited transportation made the going very difficult. Thus, Siberia gained a reputation as both a land of opportunity and a land of imprisonment.

ECONOMIC AND POLITICAL FLUCTUATIONS
IN WESTERN EUROPE

In Europe, commercialization led to increasing wealth but also heightened the risk of destabilization. Political and religious rivalries did not help.

*The Thirty Years' War*  Religious conflicts continued to rage in Europe. In Germany, Protestant and Catholic competition climaxed in the Thirty Years' War, which killed millions by 1648. The Thirty Years' War transformed warfare in Europe. Centralizing states meant bigger armies, professional soldiers, and increased use of firearms, all aimed at winning conclusive campaigns against the enemy. These and the added burden of supply lines required huge military budgets. As war became more expensive, only powerful and wealthy monarchs could win.

*Western European Economies*  Supporting armies required efficient taxation. Commerce could help, but added a new layer of competition to religious rivalries between European states. Inflation and rising costs of defense hurt Spain. Venice lost trade to new networks and thus declined. The Dutch prospered through shipping and financing of trade, setting an example to others. England and France benefited from monarch policy that protected local business while it eliminated foreign competitors. In the countryside, breakthroughs in agriculture increased food production that could support larger urban populations. Agriculture became commercialized when landowners began producing for the market, thus leading to increased efficiency and productivity.

*Dynastic Monarchies: France and England*  France employed an absolutist system. Society was represented by the Estates-General, an advisory body comprised of delegates speaking for the clergy, the nobles, and everyone else. The king, however, closed it. He ruled by divine right, and his grace and blessing were bestowed on those whom he favored. Patronage networks ultimately led to the king himself, giving him great power. Possessing all influence, the king dominated other groups who had no formal voice or representation of their interests. In practice, however, the French kings struggled to maintain their alleged "absolute" power. England developed differently because kings and queens needed Parliament for money. Fierce religious struggles led the court to clamp down with a virtual military dictatorship, but James II's intrigue to make England Catholic led to a revolution that deposed the king. Consensus was that the king's power had to be balanced by Parliament. Thus England's nobility and merchants continued to enjoy representation in Parliament. Opinions remained divided over which system was better. Thomas Hobbes supported absolutism while John Locke advocated natural rights and liberty (as Parliament represented). "Where did sovereignty ultimately rest—in the state or the people?" became a question of hot debate.

*Mercantilist Wars*  Another form of conflict arising in Europe was mercantilist war for control of colonies and sea lanes. Restrictions against foreign goods opened the door to smuggling, which became endemic. Disputed borders led to bloody conflicts, as in the Caribbean or North America. Each war exceeded the former, to the point that wars could be fought in multiple regions all at the same time, as in the Seven Years' War. That war led to the defeat of France and to British success, with France losing many of its colonies.

## QUESTIONS FOR CLASS DISCUSSION

1. How did different Europeans in North America interact with the native American peoples? Why the difference?

2. How did slaves resist or struggle against their terrible conditions?

3. What similarities can be found in the decline of the Ming, the Ottomans, and the Mughals? Were there any significant differences?

4. In what ways did Russia's eastward expansion across Siberia toward the Pacific likely reflect that of America's expansion westward toward the Pacific?

5. Contrast the French political system with that adopted by the British. Why did the two differ?

## MULTIPLE-CHOICE QUESTIONS

1. Which of the following was *not* a result of new trade routes to Asia and developing economic ties to the Americas?
   a. Even common people became subject to global economic fluctuations.
   b. Greater wealth meant countries could support larger armies.
   c. Some states became much more powerful.
   d. The standard of living for people rose everywhere across the globe.
   e. Some regimes became increasingly destabilized.

2. Mercantilist beliefs asserted that
   a. political and economic interests of the state should be kept completely separate.
   b. political interests invariably opposed economic interests.
   c. economic interests should come first, then political interests.
   d. economic interests should come last, after political interests.
   e. economic and political interests were interdependent; both should be pursued equally.

3. Mercantilists viewed colonies as
   a. existing solely for the benefit of enriching the European motherlands.
   b. a waste of effort.
   c. worth less than they cost.
   d. filled with potential for disruption and discord.
   e. great opportunities to expand national prestige and military honor.

4. Economics in the Americas relied heavily upon all of the following *except*
   a. fur trading.
   b. opium plantations.
   c. sugar plantations.
   d. tobacco plantations.
   e. slaving.

5. More than any other factor, what likely proved most deadly to slaves working on the sugar plantations?
   a. exhaustion from the grueling work day
   b. disease
   c. starvation
   d. suicide
   e. beatings and torture

6. The Dutch, French, and British respectively depended on which list to make their fortunes in the Americas?
   a. ransom, extortion, and thievery.
   b. furs, tobacco, and war.
   c. opium, slaves, and gold.
   d. trade, fur, and land.
   e. alcohol, coffee, and peanuts.

7. Many countries shipped slaves to the Americas. Who did most of the actual capturing of slaves in Africa?
   a. Africans
   b. Dutch
   c. Portuguese
   d. British
   e. Americans

8. Which of the following is *not* a feature of the Atlantic slave trade?
   a. Many more women than men were shipped to the Americas.
   b. African merchants and warlords engaged in the trade became very wealthy.
   c. Many more slaves died en route to the Americas than actually arrived there.
   d. Africa's population "hollowed out" as the number of people in the interior was depleted.
   e. The conditions facing slaves en route to the Americas were ghoulishly horrible.

9. The Dutch established themselves in the Dutch East Indies by
   a. carefully arranging treaties with the local tribal leaders.
   b. promising free trade to any interested traders in the region.
   c. destroying all competitors in order to monopolize the spice trade.
   d. destroying pirates in the region and protecting the security of all.
   e. allying with local Chinese merchants.

10. Which of the following did *not* contribute to the collapse of the Ottomans and Mughals?
    a. increasing trade opportunities with the Europeans
    b. independent-acting local elites
    c. military failures against enemies
    d. poor leadership
    e. mounting debts and other fiscal problems

11. The Qing dynasty was founded by
    a. British traders who attacked and toppled the Ming emperor.
    b. Japanese pirates who attacked and toppled the Ming emperor.
    c. Manchu mercenaries invited to China to help suppress a rebellion.
    d. Ming generals who killed the Ming emperor in a palace coup.
    e. a peasant rebel who rose to chase the Ming emperor north into Mongolia.

12. The Japanese dealt with European pressure for trade by
    a. opening to all who would come.
    b. controlling it via great naval ships.
    c. sending out pirates to disrupt the trade lanes.
    d. sealing off the country except for the port at Nagasaki.
    e. sending envoys to Europe to seek a trade treaty.

13. Which of the following developments in warfare did *not* appear by the end of the Thirty Years' War?
    a. smaller standing armies
    b. professional officer corps
    c. standardized weaponry and heavy use of gunpowder
    d. longer supply trains to support troops in the field
    e. heavy debts to pay for militaries

14. Through the 1600s, European monarchs tended to
    a. lose power to the masses.
    b. give up power to rivals in the Islamic world.
    c. gain power via centralizing measures.
    d. eschew power, preferring instead spiritual enlightenment.
    e. avoid power and its confining pressures.

15. During the eighteenth century, European wars became increasingly mercantilist. That means
    a. merchants became soldiers and fought each other.
    b. countries fought each other as they pursued colonies, control of trade routes, etc.
    c. disagreements were worked out at the negotiating table, not the battlefield.
    d. merchants refused to support governments engaged in war.
    e. wars were no longer fought with any economic objectives in mind.

## MAP EXERCISE

Looking at a map of the globe, track the spread of European colonies in Asia and the New World up to 1750. As of 1750, what areas of the globe had not yet been colonized? Why had they not yet succumbed to European expansion?

## KEYWORDS

mercantilism
Great League of Peace and
   Power
northwest passage
universal carriers
fur trade
métis
Puritans
maroon community
big whites

pawnship
pawns
Ekpe
Oyo empire
Asante state
Alafin
Dutch East India Company
Celebi revolts
Koprulu reforms
*devshirme*

Marathas
Wanli Emperor
*wokou*
roving bandits
Manchus
queue
Cohong
*samurai*
*daimyo*
*shogun*

Ezo
Muscovy
tsar
absolutist
Siberia
*fluitschips*
Thirty Years' War
Church of England
Seven Years' War

## ANSWERS TO MULTIPLE-CHOICE QUESTIONS

| | | |
|---|---|---|
| 1. d | 6. d | 11. c |
| 2. e | 7. a | 12. d |
| 3. a | 8. a | 13. a |
| 4. b | 9. c | 14. c |
| 5. a | 10. a | 15. b |

| # Cultures of Splendor and Power, 1600–1780

## CHAPTER OBJECTIVES

- To identify how borrowing and economic development led to the proliferation of culture throughout the globe
- To show how European quests for "objective" knowledge translated into power

## CHAPTER OUTLINE, CHRONOLOGY, AND SUMMARY

New World silver led to prosperity, especially in China, the Islamic empires, and Europe. New wealth greatly impacted cultural development and the spread of knowledge. Old empire cultures began to compete with new European cultural forms. European leaders tried to manage the cultural output of intellectuals.

### Trade and Culture

Culture flourished in areas profiting from the Indian Ocean and China Sea trade. Mixing and adapting became commonplace as cultures encountered each other. European cultural curiosity produced much of this contact. By the late 1700s, voyages for wealth were accompanied by voyages for knowledge of a world waiting to be cataloged, dissected, and understood. The accumulation of data led to the belief that all nature could be understood and that principles derived from it had universal applicability. Expanding long-distance trade may have helped unify the world, but culture still derived from local traditions and political needs.

### Culture in the Islamic World

Culture in the Islamic world developed as wealth expanded alongside politics as a legitimizing force for rulers. Therefore, culture in the Islamic empires assumed a degree of autonomy not seen in the Islamic cosmopolitanism of an earlier day.

THE OTTOMAN CULTURAL SYNTHESIS

Ottoman culture was a highly diverse blend that demonstrated flexibility, tolerance, and synthesis. Jews and Christians were allowed to form their own religious communities and paid a special tax for the right to do so. Recognizing that Islamic law did not address the needs of an expanding and increasingly diverse empire, the Ottoman sultans created legal codes for an empire of Muslims and non-Muslims alike. Three educational systems—for bureaucrats, scholars, and religious leaders—provided flexible institutions that helped unify the country as it prepared elites. Ottoman scholars studied religion, history, and the hard sciences, and dabbled in social science inquiry about the decline of the Ottomans. From Europe came studies of science, history, and geography, but these fell into disfavor after 1730 and did not develop a following. Celebrating life, the Ottomans became infatuated with the tulip and luxury items. Prosperity meant an abundance of all.

SAFAVID CULTURE

The Safavid Empire provided Shiism—Islam's religion of opposition—a home and a champion. To win support, however, the Safavids embraced landowners and orthodox *ulama*, thus creating a blend of Islamic Sufi brotherhoods and clerical orthodoxy, while educational institutions taught Shiite orthodoxy. With its mosques, palaces, and other buildings, Isfahan became the pinnacle of Safavid culture. Painting, carpet-weaving, tile-making, and calligraphy also reached lofty heights.

POWER AND CULTURE UNDER THE MUGHALS

In Mughal India, Muslims and Hindus alike contributed to the development of high culture, bridging religious differences.

Akbar's interest in universal truth and syncretism resulted in the production of his own religion and a model city at Fatehpur Sikri. The Taj Mahal, another example of Hindu and Muslim cooperation, combined poetry, stone, and design to produce a refined grandeur to soften Mughal military, political, and economic might. Aurangzeb showed less sympathy for non-Islamic architecture and art forms, but Mughal culture continued to thrive. Nobility consumed and enjoyed luxury items from east and west. Military units were augmented with European military personnel and technology even if the Mughals saw little use for most other European knowledge. The Islamic empires looked to China for inspiration, not Europe. Europe was viewed as a source of rivalry, not high culture.

## Culture and Politics in East Asia

In China, an expanding population and economy stimulated the spread of ideas and goods while raising new challenges for the imperial court. In Japan, the Tokugawa Shogunate struggled to control the spread of new ideas and goods.

### CHINA: THE CHALLENGE OF EXPANSION AND DIVERSITY

*Transmission of Ideas*  Between 1500 and 1700, books and ideas exploded in a publishing revolution as centralized control over printing gave way to autonomous commercialized publishing. The state simply could not control what was produced as the demand for books from elites and urban populations alike could not be satiated and unsanctioned ideas could not be contained. Connoisseurship of the arts expanded. Great libraries on a myriad of subjects grew as books and art both became affordable to a new class of urbanites. Model essays impacted the exam system, leading to complaints that memorizing, rather than learning, had become the focus but others noted the prominent role of women writers as a sign of growth.

*Popular Culture and Religion*  In rural districts, the Ming sought to maintain control over culture and behavior, appointing village elders to ensure laws and cultural norms were followed. Most peasants, however, continued to be more influenced by local Buddhist and Daoist networks or itinerant and market gossip. Thus, Ming authorities failed to monopolize cultural transmission in these networks. The secular state, however, had little reason to challenge Buddhist or Daoist institutions, provided they did not challenge the state. Thus, China enjoyed religious tolerance not seen in the west.

*Technology and Cartography*  Chinese science and technology reached new heights under the Ming. Chinese astronomers excelled, particularly since they were required to inform the emperor precisely when certain rituals had to be conducted. European science was introduced through Jesuit missionaries, who remained frustrated that Chinese did not better appreciate European contributions. Science in China, as indicated by China's own cartographic traditions, simply had a different purpose than it did in Europe. China remained relatively uninformed and disinterested in foreign lands or peoples and maintained the view that all things Chinese were superior.

### CULTURAL IDENTITY AND TOKUGAWA JAPAN

In Japan, Chinese, European, and Japanese culture interacted to stimulate cultural developments reflecting larger changes introduced by global trade. A highly refined and restrained elite culture, informed by the court and samurai class, was joined by an unrestrained, urbanite culture dominated by merchants. Popular culture rejected the principled and disciplined culture of the elites by celebrating entertainers and pleasure. Viewing the more extreme features of this culture as a threat to control and stability, the shogunate restricted it to the pleasure quarters. There, however, money ruled, allowing merchants to trump the class standing of the samurai.

Fueled by a commercializing economy and rising literacy among townspeople, publishing exploded. Through books and human contact, Chinese Chan Buddhism (called Zen in Japan) and Confucianism expanded, in part to stabilize social hierarchy and legitimize the shogunate. "Native learning," intellectual trends derived from Japan's own traditions, also thrived. Finally, the spread of European knowledge or "Dutch learning" provided Japanese with a new source of science, geography, and medicine. Unlike China or the Islamic empires, Japan showed no hesitation about borrowing ideas, systems, and knowledge from others.

## The Enlightenment in Europe

Europeans borrowed readily, but also proved eager to spread their knowledge of God and nature around the globe. This impulse came from Enlightenment views that universal and objective knowledge, gained through scientific investigation, applied to all peoples everywhere.

### ORIGINS OF THE ENLIGHTENMENT

In Europe, economic prosperity and broader cultural awareness opened the way for a new class of nonaristocrats, complete with their own sense of worth and new culture, that challenged both Europe's nobility and the church. Crises in the seventeenth century led Europe's disenchanted to seek "objective" knowledge of the world and to form new centers of culture apart from the political realm. Science and the scientific method expanded, and slowly, lower-class Europeans began to gain confidence in their own abilities to create, write, and even rule. Exposed to goods and ideas from all over the globe, European thinkers became convinced that their culture was the only true standard.

### THE NEW SCIENCE

Philosophical assertions claimed that the universe operated according to natural laws that could be understood with inductive logic and experimentation. By the end of the seventeenth century, monarchs had even begun to show interest in science as a way to augment their own power and status.

Science spread to elites outside the court and eventually to the common people, particularly as its practical value became more widely acknowledged. Even so, much of Europe remained under the influence of Christianity and the court, which had yet to be transformed by scientific "objectivity."

### ENLIGHTENMENT THINKERS

Enlightenment thinkers believed that man could be perfected, rejecting the view that man was inherently corrupt and distanced from God. Corrupted social traditions and institutions of church and state, they asserted, were the source of problems. Flourishing in Europe's cultural centers, the Enlightenment saw an explosion of printing, libraries, salons, and book clubs. Satire, which often bordered on the pornographic, criticized institutions of church and state.

Believing that men of all classes were equally endowed with reason and intelligence, Enlightenment thinkers pushed for a meritocratic system. Government should provide opportunities for all, not just elite classes. They also sought to discover, like natural scientists, the laws governing human behavior. Economic laws, claimed Adam Smith, applied to all peoples, who needed to follow them if they wanted prosperity. Turning their sights on religious practice, Enlightenment advocates demanded that religion be advanced by reason, not force. This view thus opened the way for greater toleration of religion.

Spreading ideas through the printed word, exemplified by works such as the *Encyclopedia*, Enlightenment thinkers championed rationality and commercial growth. Naturally, by this standard "Europe" fared better than most other places, creating a Euro-centric view of the world. Ironically, absolutist governments found that certain Enlightenment views could be turned to their advantage and support absolutist ambitions.

### AFRICAN CULTURAL FLOURISHING

Slave trade wealth opened the way for African elites to sponsor cultural flourishing but most activity involved local cultural forms. Art sought to glorify ruling elites by capturing energy of the spiritual realm. Asante's wealth from gold and slaves led to the production of symbolic gold-covered stools, cloth, symbols of godly power. Yoruba and Benin bronzes stand as some of the most ornate and beautifully crafted in history. In Africa, artistic forms remained relatively insulated from European influence and gained little appreciation in the Americas.

## Hybrid Cultures in the Americas

Culture in the Americas transformed as European culture blended with that of the native peoples and African slaves. Given Europe's military dominance, Amerindians and Africans adapted more of European culture than the other way around. "Civilizing" Christianity spread to Amerindians and Africans, but became hybridized as it was added to earlier religious conceptions. Colonists adapted as well, eventually becoming prosperous enough to imitate European norms even while maintaining their own unique culture.

### SPIRITUAL ENCOUNTERS

Christian missionaries in the Americas employed military and political force to win converts. Catholic missionaries in particular studied and then attacked local belief systems. Despite missionary efforts, however, conversion generally meant a form of hybridization between Christianity and local beliefs. Amerindians also had some success in converting captives or frontiersmen to local beliefs. Gender imbalances among Europeans on the frontier greatly contributed to a number of European men embracing Amerindian society, producing new hybrid peoples. Amerindianized Europeans and Christianized Amerindians both characterized and brokered the fuzzy boundary between the two groups. Relations between Africans and Europeans produced much of the same. Catholics in particular sought to Christianize slave communities, producing mixed results. Converted slaves drew inspiration from Christian hymns and stories to condemn slavery or revolt against it.

### THE MAKING OF COLONIAL CULTURES

The creoles, Spanish America's most successful hybrid culture, wrestled with their subordinate status to the "peninsulars." Discrimination and the spread of Enlightenment ideas led to the growth of creole identity and dissatisfaction with the role of the Spanish and Portuguese crowns. Published materials criticizing court policies in the New World abounded and were embraced by disenfranchised creoles.

In British America, colonists moved to emulate their motherland elites by building huge estates embellished with finery from all over the world. Great numbers of books drew Americans into the Enlightenment craze as both consumers and producers of such works as the Declaration of Independence.

## Imperialism in Oceania

As Europeans pressed into the far reaches of Oceania, Australia became Anglicized. Largely separate from other world cultures, Australia had developed on its own, home to hunter-gatherers. Parts of Oceania had already been claimed by European colonists. By the late eighteenth century, these people were ready to move to Australia.

### THE SCIENTIFIC VOYAGES OF CAPTAIN COOK

Engaging in a form of scientific imperialism—the pursuit of power through the pursuit of knowledge—James Cook opened the South Pacific to Europeans. Armed with scientists and equipment, his expedition studied and recorded flora, fauna, geography, and people, accounts of which were celebrated in Europe. European plans for Australia meant its transformation. Eager to begin, Cook brought European animals and plants to make the land more receptive to European colonists. Eastern Australia was designated as a prison colony and as a supplier of natural resources. As in the Americas, European expansion came at the expense of the native peoples. European knowledge, in like manner, also came at native peoples' expense, as witnessed by the practice of kidnapping them to show them off in Europe.

CLASSIFICATION AND "RACE"

By the late seventeenth century, science's classification of nature was applied to humans, and the term "race" entered the vocabulary of Europeans. To each so-called race were attached certain features and characteristics that, often but not always, placed Europeans at the top of a new racial hierarchy and Africans at the bottom. While classifications of the peoples of Oceania originally described them as innocent and peace loving, Cook's violent death and other incidents led Europeans to depict them as cruel savages.

## QUESTIONS FOR CLASS DISCUSSION

1. Could it be said that increased contact between various parts of the globe led to a global culture combining elements of all?

2. What happened to European culture when it began to encounter cultures in other parts of the globe?

3. In what ways did economic growth across the globe contribute to changes in culture?

4. Culturally, what distinguished the Ottomans, the Chinese, and the Mughals from the Europeans?

5. What similarities exist between the Japanese willingness to borrow from other cultures and the European views about the world beyond Europe's borders?

## MULTIPLE-CHOICE QUESTIONS

1. Which of the following statements about cultural flourishing in the seventeenth and eighteenth centuries is most true?
   a. All cultures eagerly borrowed from all others.
   b. Chinese culture set the standard for the whole globe.
   c. Most cultures abandoned their own ways for those of the Europeans.
   d. The major cultures borrowed from others, but still viewed their own ways as superior.
   e. World cultures refused to borrow from others.

2. Culturally, the Ottomans were
   a. flexible, relatively tolerant, and diverse.
   b. anxious to create a single culture that all people adopted as their own.
   c. eager to tolerate all but Christians in their boundaries.
   d. quick to crush religious diversity within the empire.
   e. highly intolerant of minority viewpoints or cultures.

3. Safavid culture displayed all *but* which of the following?
   a. a commitment to Shiism
   b. loyalty to the Safavid family
   c. powerful religious institutions
   d. a highly developed appreciation for Catholic ritual
   e. miniature paintings, tile mosaics, and calligraphy

4. Which of the following is *not* an element of Mughal India at its cultural apex?
   a. the Akbarnamah (or Book of Akbar)
   b. strict rejection of all Hindu culture
   c. miniature paintings
   d. the Taj Mahal
   e. the hybridization of Hindu and Muslim art forms

5. At their apex, the Mughals
   a. absorbed and adopted European military technology.
   b. rejected all European military technology.
   c. feared European military technology.
   d. lost to European military technology.
   e. abandoned their own military technology in favor of Europe's.

6. Which of the following is *not* an element of Ming culture in its last one hundred years?
   a. an explosion of printing
   b. popularity of Buddhist and Daoist sects among the common people
   c. a highly developed understanding of astronomy
   d. the introduction of Christianity through Jesuit missionaries
   e. a stoic form of theater called No, based on China's warrior elite class

7. China avoided the religious warfare of post-Reformation Europe because
   a. common Chinese were not religious.
   b. Chinese religion is tolerant because it is syncretic, diffused, and decentralized.
   c. the government intervened to stop religious wars from escalating.
   d. Chinese Protestants and Catholics hated each other but refused to fight.
   e. China did not avoid religious wars.

8. In the days of the Tokugawa Shogunate, Japanese culture represented a composite that blended elements of
   a. European, Chinese, and Ottoman cultures.
   b. Chinese, Southeast Asian, and Japanese cultures.
   c. Ottoman, Mughal, and Japanese cultures.
   d. Japanese, European, and Chinese cultures.
   e. African, Chinese, and Japanese cultures.

9. Which of the following is *not* an accurate statement about culture during the Enlightenment?
   a. Europeans categorically refused to borrow from all other cultures.
   b. Literacy, education, and printing in Europe greatly advanced.
   c. Nonaristocrats (lawyers, doctors, etc.) showed great enthusiasm for science and the arts.
   d. Europeans began to show greater appreciation for the sciences.
   e. Philosophers began to emphasize merit rather than birth as indicative of a person's worth.

10. European interest in science appeared first and foremost within which group?
    a. peasants
    b. workers
    c. military men
    d. the court and educated aristocracy
    e. clergy

11. Which of the following is *not* an example of Enlightenment thinking?
    a. Birth should not determine one's status.
    b. All people possess worth because they have been endowed with reason.
    c. Ideas come from experience.
    d. Inequalities between philosophers and street porters exist due to differences in opportunity.
    e. Because of their high birth, aristocrats are more highly favored by God and thus privileged.

12. African arts
    a. glorified royal power and captured spiritual energy.
    b. were produced strictly for the market.
    c. always doubled as weapons of war.
    d. were traded for slaves and horses.
    e. became quite popular in Europe during the 1700s.

13. Which of the following statements best represents attempts to Christianize America's Indian population?
    a. These attempts led to complete and utter failure—no Indians became Christian.
    b. These attempts led to tremendous conflicts as Indians accepted Christianity but not the church.
    c. These attempts led to a hybridization or mixture of Christian and Indian beliefs.
    d. These attempts led to problems, since only a very few missionaries were willing to teach the Indians.
    e. These attempts led to complete success—all Indians became Christian.

14. Captain James Cook is known for all of the following *except*
    a. embarking on long explorations to the South Pacific.
    b. refusing to capture native peoples and returning them to Europe for study.
    c. dedicating his life to science.
    d. transplanting European flora and fauna to South Pacific islands.
    e. getting killed in Hawaii.

15. In their quest to understand and classify the world, early European anthropologists began to divide the world's populations into
    a. religions.
    b. countries.
    c. genders.
    d. races.
    e. nationalities.

## MAP EXERCISE

Looking at a map of the globe, identify places where European culture had the most impact. Where did Islamic-inspired culture have the most impact? Where did Chinese-inspired culture have the most impact?

## KEYWORDS

| | |
|---|---|
| gunpowder empires | *shamisen* |
| *dhimmis* | *kabuki* |
| *millets* | *ukiyo* |
| *jizya* | *ukiyo-e* |
| *kanun* | *jinsei* |
| *sharia* | native learning |
| *madrasas* | *tabula rasa* |
| *qadis* | invisible hand |
| *muftis* | *mestizos* |
| *tekkes* | *métis* |
| the tulip period | *Santeria* |
| *kizilbash* | *vodun* |
| *takkiyas* | *candomblé* |
| *Akbarnamah* | big houses |
| Taj Mahal | the *Endeavour* |
| eight-legged essay | *Homo sapiens* |
| devils | *Homo caudatus* |
| Dutch learning | *Homo troglodytes* |
| Nō drama | |

## ANSWERS TO MULTIPLE-CHOICE QUESTIONS

| | | |
|---|---|---|
| 1. d | 6. e | 11. e |
| 2. a | 7. b | 12. a |
| 3. d | 8. d | 13. c |
| 4. b | 9. a | 14. b |
| 5. a | 10. d | 15. d |

# CHAPTER 15 | Reordering the World, 1750–1850

## CHAPTER OBJECTIVES

- To describe the spread of revolutionary ideas and models around the globe
- To describe how economics changed, particularly in Europe and Africa
- To demonstrate how some cultures began to decline while others began to expand

## CHAPTER OUTLINE, CHRONOLOGY, AND SUMMARY

The hundred years after 1750 marked a profound restructuring of world power. Political and economic changes in the Atlantic world impacted Asia and Africa as the power of Europe expanded.

### Revolutionary Transformations and New Languages of Freedom

Dissatisfied with their exclusion from power and wealth, politically aware people began organizing in hopes that a new or reformed system would provide freedom to trade and representation in government. Initially unwilling to revolt, these reformers found powerful resistance among the aristocracy. Arguing for popular sovereignty and free trade, they denounced trade monopolies and aristocratic domination of politics. New identities and concepts of "nation" arose. The question of how much freedom and to whom, however, generally meant for white males only.

### Political Reorderings

As Enlightenment ideals spread, certain groups in the colonies began seeking a new relationship with their respective motherlands. More sought involvement in politics and claimed to serve the interests of the "people." Ideas like independence, freedom, and equality had power and prompted political revolts in the Americas and Europe. Since then revolution has been a powerful force.

### THE NORTH AMERICAN WAR OF INDEPENDENCE, 1776–1783

Competition over land between estate owners and small farmers pushed American colonists into the interior where they fell into conflict with Amerindian peoples. Aligning with the French, Amerindians battled the British, but lost their ally when France was defeated in the Seven Years' War. Seeking to make the colonies pay for the war against France, King George III moved to restrain American smuggling and raise taxes. War broke out, encouraging talk of independence from England and the writing of the Declaration of Independence.

As they fought, Americans began constructing a new government system. Elections produced delegates to represent the "people"—head-of-household landowners. Women and slaves participated in the war, believing they would be rewarded for their efforts with greater freedoms. Landed elites, however, convened the Constitutional Convention to prevent the revolution from falling into anarchy. There the new federal government was empowered and the power of the legislature was reduced to moderate the popular will. The Constitution and a Bill of Rights formed the basis for government.

New lands deflected the slave issue but the problem did not go away. For the moment, white elites maintained their privilege by suppressing black uprisings.

### THE FRENCH REVOLUTION, 1789–1799

Also inspired by Enlightenment ideas, the French Revolution had global impact. In France, peasant suffering and widespread hostility toward the court, aristocracy, and church raised tensions. Visions of an Enlightenment-based polity and France's extraordinary fiscal problems opened the door for revolution. Sustaining huge debts in support of the American bid for independence, the French court convened the Estates-General in order to raise taxes. The Third Estate (wealthy commoners), however, condemned the nobles and clergy as parasites and formed the National Assembly—a body claiming to speak for the people of France.

After news spread of the storming of the Bastille, crowds attacked aristocratic manors and records of feudal dues with such ferocity that frightened aristocrats renounced their privileges. The "Declaration of the Rights of Man and Citizen" championed individual rights and the right of the people to representative government. Women were granted some rights, but not equal to men. As aristocracy fled the country, the Revolution splintered into factions with the more radical Jacobins eventually taking control. They executed the king and launched a Reign of Terror to rid France of counterrevolutionaries. Universal conscription made the Revolution's armies the world's largest and spread revolutionary ideas to other parts of Europe. The transformation of France into a revolutionary system led to new names, times, and even religion.

With time, however, enthusiasm for the radicals heading the Revolution waned and was eclipsed by the rise of Napoleon. Napoleon's reign marked a return to more moderate policies. The bloodletting ended. Catholicism returned. A new constitution and legal system were adopted.

## NAPOLEON'S EMPIRE, 1799–1815

French expansion into neighboring states was accompanied by promises of liberty for those who supported the revolutionary armies. As French successes mounted, however, many so-called liberated peoples began to resist. Even as Napoleon sought to unify Europe, he awakened nationalism in people, such as the Germans, who had little cause to notice it before. A world war developed as Napoleon struggled against all of Europe's powers. Forced to retreat from Moscow, Napoleon was defeated at Paris and later Waterloo, and dreams of a French empire collapsed.

At the Congress of Vienna, Europe's old aristocratic interests moved to build a new order capable of meeting the revolutionary threat. Rejecting the option of a constitution, the Congress based itself on a system of mutual support and balancing power politics. The French monarchy was restored. While France seemed to have returned to its former self, German and Italian principalities began to unify, upsetting the Congress of Vienna's balance of power.

## REVOLUTIONS IN THE CARIBBEAN AND IBERIAN AMERICA

Revolution soon spread, spearheaded by people of color in the lowest classes. Andean Indians rose up against Cuzco. Such energy prompted colonial elites to support their respective crowns in Iberia until the Napoleonic wars severed those ties. Elites suppressed revolution among the lower classes. Only in Haiti did slaves succeed.

*Revolution in Saint Domingue (Haiti)* Following events in France, white settlers called for independence while slaves sought emancipation. Civil war ensued. Slaves fought French, British, and Spanish forces, and then Toussaint L'Ouverture's forces destroyed Napoleon's army, which was sent to restore slavery and order. Most revolutionary nations, like the new United States, refused to recognize Haiti.

*Brazil and Constitutional Monarchy* Avoiding Napoleon by fleeing to Brazil, the Portuguese royal family reformed Brazilian society and preempted calls for independence, since Brazil was now the center of their empire. When the king left and Brazilian elites threatened to overthrow the crown, however, the prince declared Brazil independent. Brazil's elites conspired to keep the lower orders in their place, preserving stability and crushing any movement that arose to challenge them.

*Mexico's Independence* With the Spanish king under Napoleon's control, Spanish America had to govern itself, developing autonomy in the process. When the crown again sought to assert control over the colonies, they resisted and pursued independence on the model of Enlightenment ideals as seen elsewhere. Royal troops kept the peace until a popular movement based on peasants threatened creoles and royalists alike. When Spanish control in Spain declined, the army sided with the creoles, and Mexican independence was declared.

*Other South American Revolutions* Despite commitment to Enlightenment ideals and rule by reason, the revolution led by Bolívar in Venezuela and San Martín in Argentina became bloody affairs. Revolution martialized the lower classes, which sought liberation from oppression of the elite landed classes. As class conflict broke out, civil war ensued, and the region broke into segments. Ideas of unity gave way to the realities of local need and interest. Bolívar's hope for a unified confederation fell apart. Ultimately, regional military chieftains emerged as the real victors.

## Change and Trade in Africa

Revolution also visited Africa, but primarily as a result of rising wealth and the demise of the slave trade, rather than Enlightenment views.

### ABOLITION OF THE SLAVE TRADE

In the late eighteenth century, abolitionists condemned slave trading as immoral and organized themselves to ensure its end. One by one, European powers banned the trade. Britain then sent naval forces to enforce the ban off the coast of West Africa and to pressure the Brazilians to cease importing slaves. Some illegal slaving continued, but slave ships were harassed by British squadrons. Rescued Africans were repatriated to Sierra Leone or Liberia.

European traders then turned their interests to Africa's natural resources and agricultural products, like vegetable oils. European interest came partly in the hope that trade would stimulate Africa's economy and better enable Africans to afford European manufactures. Plantations did not impact the environment as heavily as in the Caribbean, but eventually did lead to desertification when forests were felled. In some cases, African merchants became extremely wealthy and produced a body of educated and wealthy elites able to engage in politics. Others, more closely aligned to the old slaving networks, found their income compromised, and either adapted or fell apart.

The rise of plantations in Africa, however, did not mean the collapse of slavery as an institution. Slaves were now owned by Africans, who employed their labor on agricultural plantations owned by Arabs or Swahili big men. Slaves were also used in military forces to the point that in some areas slaves comprised half of the total population.

## Economic Reordering

Changes in the Atlantic world opened the way for the Industrial Revolution, shattered the old mercantilist system, and made Western Europe and North America the wealthiest and most powerful of world powers.

### BRITAIN'S ECONOMIC LEADERSHIP

Coal, iron, new technologies, capital, internal markets, water transportation, and labor all contributed to Britain's industrial development. Improvements in agriculture allowed it to feed more people and thus sustain larger cities, swelling with the surplus of a rising population. Peasants, cut off from the land, became laborers in the workshops of the cities, which turned raw materials from the colonies into manufactured goods. This economic change transformed the way people lived.

### TRADING AND FINANCING

Ingredients or services from all parts of the globe drew together to form new products, such as tea and soap. The scale was such that even the poorer classes could afford imported goods. Merchants garnered immense fortunes, while lawyers, insurance agents, and financiers profited handsomely. Those enriched by commerce became the bourgeoisie. Eager to expand their influence, the bourgeoisie established ties with each other and began competing with the aristocratic class. Most bourgeoisie arose from the ranks of commoners, some becoming extremely powerful, like the Rothschilds.

As world trade led to greater integration of the world economy, these leaders sought to streamline economic relations and open trade in order to provide better opportunities. Political power and laws became the means to push for free trade, particularly when foreign countries employed protectionist policies or used high tariffs to protect their farmers or other interests. The Americas initiated a drive to establish free trade relations with Europe: Latin America abolished protectionist tariffs, and the United States opened trade as well, but stopped somewhat short by refusing to allow cheap British goods to compete with locally produced goods. Europe, especially Britain, enjoyed inexpensive food items and raw materials as open markets and free trade became a guiding principle.

### MANUFACTURING

As technical know-how developed among small operations in the countryside and then spread, it snowballed. Inventors, like James Watt who improved the steam engine, linked up with industrialists, thus combining thinking and producing. Improvements in steam engines and iron production, which opened the way for railways, steam-driven ships, and iron bridges, greatly cut distances. Textile production replaced home handicrafts and improved the quality and quantity of cloth. The cotton gin accelerated production of raw cotton, providing British looms with enough cheap cotton that the prices of shirts dropped considerably. By the middle of the nineteenth century, industrialization had spread to other northern European countries, but these still lagged far behind the British. There, agriculture still dominated.

### WORKING AND LIVING

Industrialization meant that factory laborers as well as farmers and slaves worked harder. It also stimulated urbanization and great, but unhealthy, cities emerged, especially in England. Parents and children contributed wages to the family. Most jobs meant long hours for all, including women and children. New commitments to time schedules and rigid work disciplines emerged. Labor often produced poor wages and numbing drudgery. Unemployment, however, was worse, and the unemployed were forced to work in workhouses under terrible conditions. Industrialization, while increasing production, also destroyed age-old handicraft industries and abused a new class of laborers, giving rise to social problems and new legislation. In short, life had changed.

## Persistence and Change in Afro-Eurasia

Economic reordering and revolution in the Atlantic world stimulated the old systems of Russia, China, and the Ottoman Empire to strengthen but not remake themselves. Changes in all three allowed them to survive into the twentieth century, but also taught that the world ran on a different set of principles that could not be ignored.

REVAMPING THE RUSSIAN MONARCHY

Defeating Napoleon allowed the tsar of Russia to glorify himself and those who fought in the war, but it also spread new ideas that sorely undercut the tsar's absolutist system. When he died in 1825, army officers from elite families seeking change supported Constantine in the hope of getting a constitution for Russia. When Constantine supported Nicholas as heir, the reform-minded Decembrists were crushed. Grappling with new ideas of popular sovereignty and constitutions spilling over from other countries, the tsar justified his position by proclaiming himself the historical embodiment of the nation while adding healthy doses of suppression. Secret police, however, could not work alone and were aided by a new conservative ideology that sought to romanticize the Russian heritage and thereby to legitimize the tsar's position. Reform went nowhere.

REFORMING EGYPT AND THE OTTOMAN EMPIRE

Napoleon brought successes and ideas that challenged Ottoman rulers beyond even economic changes already affecting their empire. Reformist calls became commonplace. In Egypt, Muhammad Ali quickly adopted European modernizing institutions and systems. He built a modern army using French advisers and officers, reformed education and medicine, and improved agriculture. His reforms, however, pressured locals caught up in the faster pace of modernization and engendered local resistance. Military successes caught the eye of concerned Ottoman and British leaders who forced Ali to reduce his forces.

Worried about Egyptian and European strength and angered at the weakness of his own forces, Sultan Selim III moved to build a New Order military force, but it and his power were crushed in a coup headed by janissary and *ulama* interests. Military and religious interests thus blocked reform at the top until Mahmud II used clerical and popular support to crush the janissaries and institute sweeping changes. Unfortunately for Mahmud, the reforms stopped short of transforming agriculture, financing, or the Ottomans' old administration. By the nineteenth century, the Ottomans had even lost control of international trade to Europeans.

COLONIAL REORDERING IN INDIA

Unlike the economy of North America, India's economy fell increasingly under the control of the British, specifically the English East India Company. What started as a strictly commercial interest, soon began to involve politics when British troops took Delhi. Seizing taxation rights and annexing great portions of India, British control expanded to exceed even that of the Mughals. Hindu and Muslim princes became administrators overseeing the job of running the country along with the Company's own centralized bureaucracy. To maintain its privileged position, the Company kept its own army.

British influence increased. Orientalist scholars studied India's past, languages, religions, and peoples, allowing the Company to present itself as a supporter of Hindu culture. The Company land-tax system greatly increased Company revenues while also stripping land from those unable to pay. Urbanization rose. Colonial cities, geared toward trade, began to supplant those that had once dominated India from the interior. Eager to share the Company's success, other British interests complained about the Company's monopolization of Indian wealth and production. After the Company's abolition in 1813, India began to be viewed more and more as a market for British textiles, thus destroying India's own budding industrialization and reversing its balance of trade. Accompanying this was a shift in attitude about India in general. To justify further British control, James and John Stuart Mill attacked India's cultural traditions, claiming that only autocratic government could work in India. Missionaries condemned Hindu and Muslim social practices. British administrators applauded British cultural superiority. All moved to create a class of Indians with British education and tastes.

Many Indians rankled under British rule, which restricted their activities and opportunities. Nevertheless, British authority expanded.

PERSISTENCE OF THE QING EMPIRE

Enjoying continued prosperity and expansion, the Qing remained disinterested in revolutionary changes taking place elsewhere.

*Expansion of the Empire* The Qing enjoyed a powerful military, which extended China's boundaries, and the fruits of New World crops, which helped stimulate agricultural production. Commercialization spread as the population rose. Peasant handicrafts industries spread.

*Problems of the Empire* Population growth, however, began to pinch resources even as the Qing court moved slowly to deal with changes. The tax system remained vulnerable to abuse and corruption. Rebellions arose. Despite problems, China continued as a strong and dominant power so long as Chinese goods continued to be extremely popular in Europe.

*The Opium War and the "Opening" of China* Opium, however, changed everything. In greater and greater numbers, Chinese accustomed to tobacco began to use opium brought by Europeans. Although the Qing court banned the drug, usage spread. Seeking to trade opium for tea, the East India Company induced Indian peasants to raise opium, which could then be shipped to China. Enormous quantities of opium made their way to China, swelled by the number of merchants involved. By the 1820s, the value of opium coming into China exceeded the value of goods exported out. Thus, the Chinese had to pay silver in addition to their goods to get opium. Silver shortages began to hurt peasants.

until foreign merchants handed over their opium stores. The opium traders eventually complied, giving Lin a short-lived victory. In 1840, however, British naval ships attacked and subdued Qing forces. The resulting Treaty of Nanjing gave Hong Kong to Britain and broke up China's restrictions on foreign trade by opening new treaty ports. It also exempted foreigners from Chinese law and gave Britain any privileges that any other European nation might gain in the future. Although China remained under the emperor's rule, foreign influence began to spread into the coastal areas and the cities.

## QUESTIONS FOR CLASS DISCUSSION

1. Does the phrase "liberty and justice for all" adequately describe the revolutions of the late eighteenth century? How might it apply? How might it not apply? Might the phrase mean different things to different people?

2. How might Napoleon's conquests have contributed to the rise of nationalism in other, surrounding countries? Why didn't other peoples just accept French dominance?

3. What impact did the rise of manufacturing have on European society? How did things change after factories became commonplace?

4. What did the Russians do to revive their country? Why couldn't the Ottomans do the same things?

5. Why was the Opium War significant? What impact did it have on the economic and political power of the combatants?

## MULTIPLE-CHOICE QUESTIONS

1. All of the following contributed to the North American War of Independence *except*
   a. the British crown's attempt to make the colonies pay for the Seven Years' War.
   b. the British crown's attempt to stamp out smuggling among the colonists.
   c. the British crown's attempt to tax colonists without allowing representation in Parliament.
   d. new ideas about the rights of citizens to good government and what good government was.
   e. the British crown's commitment to policies reflecting the ideals of "liberty for all."

2. "Freedom for all" failed to include all of the following *except*
   a. women.
   b. slaves.
   c. land-owning white males.
   d. farmers following Daniel Shays.
   e. female slaves.

3. All of the following contributed to the French Revolution *except*
   a. heavy debts from France's support for the American colonies' war against England.
   b. a growing resentment among the French toward corruption in the church and court.
   c. increasing popularity of the view that social place was fixed by God and not to be disputed.
   d. the storming of the Bastille on July 14, 1789.
   e. the example of the American Revolution.

4. Radical control over the French Revolution led to
   a. increasing freedoms for all underprivileged French people.
   b. execution of the king and tens of thousands of other French men and women.
   c. demilitarization of France.
   d. increased peace and prosperity throughout the land.
   e. a new republic much like that founded by the Americans.

5. Symbols and innovations associated with revolutionary France included all *but* which of the following?
   a. a new god or Supreme Being
   b. new street names
   c. a new flag
   d. new statues honoring the royal family
   e. the practice of addressing each other as "citizen"

6. The beginning of Napoleon's swift decline came with a loss to
   a. Britain.
   b. Russia.
   c. France.
   d. Germany.
   e. Japan.

7. Many would argue that Napoleon's most significant contribution to world history was
   a. the impact his troops had in sparking nationalistic sentiment throughout Europe.
   b. the establishment of a huge French empire.
   c. his failed campaign against Egypt.
   d. his disastrous attempt to conquer Russia.
   e. his success in winning the hearts of his countrymen.

8. Most of Latin America's successful revolutions were dominated by elite men of pure or mixed European descent. One that succeeded in liberating slaves was fought in
   a. Mexico.
   b. Brazil.
   c. Saint Domingue (Haiti).
   d. Florida.
   e. Argentina.

9. As trade accelerated, merchants and financiers began to recognize the greater potential of free trade. The first countries to actually implement free-trade practice were
   a. Britain and France.
   b. Japan and China.
   c. Russia and Finland.
   d. the New World countries, particularly Latin America.
   e. the United States and Australia.

10. As the slave trade across the Atlantic declined
   a. slavery as an institution completely ended.
   b. slavery increased in the Americas.
   c. slavery remained strong in Africa itself.
   d. slaves in Africa were released from bondage.
   e. all slaves in the Americas returned to Africa.

11. Workers in British factories suffered for all of the following reasons *except*
   a. commodities became somewhat cheaper to buy.
   b. work days often extended to twelve or more hours.
   c. severe pollution became commonplace.
   d. clocks and bells could be manipulated to cheat workers of their own time.
   e. workers often received very low wages.

12. Egypt's Muhammad Ali reformed his country by instituting all *but* which of the following changes?
   a. modernizing reforms in the military
   b. the construction of engineering schools
   c. a new medical campus in Cairo
   d. cultural transformations designed to strengthen Christianity
   e. irrigating canals and dams

13. As British influence in Mughal India expanded, the Mughal emperor
   a. was killed in a British artillery bombardment.
   b. was left on his throne to maintain much of the civil administration of India.
   c. fled the country to Tibet where he organized resistance against the British.
   d. abdicated in favor of the British crown.
   e. refused to appear at court and was forgotten.

14. Qing China's official response to British requests for open-trading practices was
   a. to welcome foreign trade with open arms.
   b. graciously decline out of respect for the ancestors.
   c. to cautiously agree to further commercial contact.
   d. angrily denounce the British for being greedy.
   e. declare that China had no use for Europe's manufactured goods.

15. The Opium War involved
   a. India's refusal to grow opium because of its moral implications.
   b. a conflict between Britain and China over opium production in Hong Kong.
   c. Britain's willingness to militarily support the right of merchants to sell opium to China.
   d. a conflict between British and Chinese armies, both of which used opium.
   e. China's eagerness to gain back a village named "Opium."

## MAP EXERCISE

Looking at a map of the globe, identify where revolutions first began to break out. Explain why they erupted in these locations rather than elsewhere in the world.

## KEYWORDS

| | |
|---|---|
| *liberté* | guerrillas |
| *egalité* | Congress of Vienna |
| freeborn Englishmen | Black Jacobin |
| Declaration of Independence | *gauchos* |
| natural rights | creoles |
| Constitutional Convention | peninsulars |
| Federalists | Virgin of Guadalupe |
| Anti-Federalists | *caudillos* |
| Bill of Rights | the great divide |
| Shays' rebellion | bourgeoisie |
| Estates-General | Corn Laws |
| Third Estate | entrepreneurs |
| Declaration of the Rights of Man and Citizen | Decembrists |
| | *bilharzia* |
| National Assembly | *Tanzimat* |
| Girondins | *sipahi* |
| Jacobins | *sati* |
| Reign of Terror | Orientalists |
| *patria* | Asiatic Society |
| Directory | White Lotus Rebellion |
| Code Napoleon | *chinoiserie* |
| | Opium War |

## ANSWERS TO MULTIPLE-CHOICE QUESTIONS

| | |
|---|---|
| 1. e | 9. d |
| 2. c | 10. c |
| 3. c | 11. a |
| 4. b | 12. d |
| 5. d | 13. b |
| 6. b | 14. e |
| 7. a | 15. c |
| 8. c | |

# CHAPTER 16

# Alternative Visions of the Nineteenth Century

## CHAPTER OBJECTIVES

- To depict the global rise of prophets and to describe their alternative visions to secular modernity
- To portray popular movements resistant to colonizing and centralizing states

## CHAPTER OUTLINE, CHRONOLOGY, AND SUMMARY

Prophetic crusades of the nineteenth century, such as Wovoka's Ghost Dancers, rose to challenge the spread of a modernity featuring French and American revolutionary ideals, capitalism, nation-states, technology, and industry.

### Reactions to Social and Political Change

By the nineteenth century, changes across the globe had deeply disrupted older orders. As societies changed and secularized, many questioned the value of moving into a new Western-dominated world. The spectrum of alternatives ranged widely. Some struggled to fend off Western influence even though they avoided direct colonization. Others, especially marginalized Europeans, found themselves caught in the middle of tremendous change and sought a Socialist solution. Still others wrestled with colonization. All opposed authority and drew inspiration from cultural traditions to protect their local communities. At the same time, all proposed change as they struggled to redefine their new role on the edges of the developing world.

### Prophecy and Revitalization in the Islamic World and Africa

Western-styled reform and economic development in the Islamic heartland spawned resentment along the edges of the Islamic world. It also stimulated reaction in non-Islamic Africa. Alarmed that Christian European influence was encroaching upon their societies, religious leaders arose to call for revitalization of traditional culture.

ISLAMIC REVITALIZATION

Revitalization rejected westernization, proposing instead theocratic polities to implement Allah's will, fight unbelievers, and purify Islamic culture. The Wahhabi Movement targeted the secularizing Ottoman state by demanding a return to "pure" Islam and attacking any who would not follow. Not persuaded, the Egyptians helped suppress the disturbances. In West Africa, the Fulani produced similar responses, particularly that of Usman dan Fodio's movement, which challenged the Hausa rulers and spread Islam throughout norther Nigeria. With the support of warrior women and educated women, the Fulani became very successful in Nigeria.

CHARISMATIC MILITARY MEN AND
PROPHETS IN NON-ISLAMIC AFRICA

Non-Islamic Africa also saw new political movements although they were not based on religion so much as "big men" traditions. Employing fear, violence, and discipline, Shaka's centralized Zulu state was so successful against enemies that other states were forced to centralize their power. Incorporating defeated peoples into his own system, Shaka successfully expanded clan and ethnic ties. With time, central and southern Africa came to host large polities that reshaped the political landscape.

### Prophecy and Rebellion in China

Rising Western influence in China, reversing economic fortunes, and social problems associated with the opium trade all signaled the Qing's inability to curb foreign influence. Sensing China was due for a change, Hong Xiuquan moved to restore China's greatness by rejecting the Confucian order in favor of one based on quasi-Christian ideals and Buddhist/Daoist views of egalitarianism and millenarianism.

### THE DREAM

After failing the Confucian exam, Hong dreamed of an encounter with various heavenly figures and personalities. Connecting this experience with Christian beliefs, Hong interpreted it to mean that God the Father and Jesus Christ had commanded him to rid the world of evil and demons.

### THE REBELLION

Calling for a restored society of egalitarianism and justice, Hong built a following among poor and marginalized Chinese. Gradually Hong's followers blamed the Qing Manchu "demons" that infested China, attacked the government, and destroyed icons of Confucianism. Tens of thousands joined Hong's movement and its new social order, which was based on Bible teachings, equality of the sexes, common property, and strict restrictions on "indulgences." Qing efforts to defeat the Taipings in 1850 only dislodged them, precipitating a bloody trek to Nanjing where they ruled for ten years before falling to factionalism and combined Qing and Western forces. Although the Taiping movement did not last, the impulse to form an alternative and just order did.

## Utopians, Socialists, and Radicals in Europe

In Europe, political, social, cultural, and religious prophets rose in great numbers to challenge the dominance of monarchical-conservatives associated with the Congress of Vienna system.

### RESTORATION AND RESISTANCE

After Napoleon, Europe hosted a wide variety of new ideologies. Those, plus a long tradition of religious radicalism, provided inspiring material from which to construct alternative visions of remaking European society. "Reactionaries," like the Slavophiles, moved to reverse all the democratic and secularizing influences introduced by the French Revolution and Napoleonic era. "Liberals," like John Stuart Mill, sought to preserve order by limiting state power while expanding that of the individual.

### RADICAL VISIONS

"Radicals" wanted a total reconstruction of society in favor of one based on popular sovereignty, a prospect that frightened liberals and reactionaries into an uncomfortable alliance.

*Nationalists* "Nationalists," who sought national sovereignty from the Russian, Prussian, Austrian, and Ottoman empires that controlled them, proved the least offensive form of radicals. Greek nationalists succeeded, albeit somewhat short of their goals; most others failed under the heavy hand of anxious monarchs fearful that revolutionary energies had returned.

*Socialists and Communists* Radicals such as Communists and Socialists pursued transformation of the economic order, dismantling of the free market system, and destruction of aristocratic privilege as a means of rectifying social problems among the poor. Despite widespread popular support, efforts to petition change from Britain's parliament failed to gain political sanction.

*Fourier and Utopian Socialism* Utopian Socialism, such as that of Charles Fourier who sought to eliminate market injustice, also failed to gain headway despite articulate planning and vision. Fourier's sharp critique of commercial society stimulated a generation of other radicals, including Karl Marx, who eventually did have an impact.

*Marxism* The theories of Marx and Engels, which traced economic exploitation through history, hotly condemned capitalism and predicted the emergence of a Socialist order featuring equality, liberty, and fraternity under a dictatorship of the proletariat. Although unsuccessful in his personal quest to hasten the emergence of this new world order, Marx did produce a vision that remained vibrant and persuasive to many.

## Insurgencies against Colonizing and Centralizing States

In colonized regions, native peoples turned to prophets, rebellion, and charismatic leaders for ways to respond to changes transforming their local communities. As in China and the Islamic world, inspiration combined traditions of the past with completely new visions of modernity.

### ALTERNATIVE TO THE EXPANDING UNITED STATES: NATIVE AMERICAN PROPHETS

Concerned about the future, many Indians followed Shawnee prophet Tenskwatawa who foretold the white man's disappearance if Indians returned to traditional rites. Like other movements, including one among the Pueblo villagers of New Mexico and another headed by Neolin, those attracted to Tenskwatawa hated the thought of changing into farmers. Visions and preaching attracted allies in a large Indian confederation but alarmed white authorities in the process. Military failure and the death of Tenskwatawa's brother Tecumseh led to the collapse of the movement and the eventual expulsion of Amerindian peoples from the Ohio Valley.

### ALTERNATIVE TO THE CENTRAL STATE: THE CASTE WAR OF YUCATAN

The expanding Mexican state prompted responses such as the Mayan revolt in the Yucatan. While affected only moderately by Spanish conquests and trading networks, the Mayans of the Yucatan struggled with a new class of white elites who dominated through sugar plantations, tax collecting, and conscription. In 1847, a popular uprising called the Caste War broke out, alarming whites. Whites were nearly driven out of the Yucatan before the arrival of the planting season caused the Mayan fighters to return home. When the war with the United States stopped, the Mexican government sent forces south and viciously crushed the movement. A residual point of resistance coalesced at Santa Cruz (Little Holy Cross), where Christian ritual and traditional Mayan beliefs blended. With time, however, the Mayan resistance could not adapt economically and its adherents were forced to work on plantations. Thus, the alternative vision of the Mayans succumbed to military pressures and hunger.

THE REBELLION OF 1857 IN INDIA

In India, contact with British colonialism stimulated native uprisings that climaxed in 1857. As in cases elsewhere, the rebels built on community loyalty and tradition to foster support for an egalitarian alternative to British dominance. Consolidating its power, the East India Company began to strip Indian aristocracy of their influence and to tax peasants directly. Replacing Indian elites as the administrators, the British began modernization programs that included the industry, military, and infrastructure needed to create a modern state.

Sparked by the "greased cartridge" controversy, Indian troops revolted, slaughtered British officers, and restored the Mughal emperor. Asserting Hindu and Muslim unity, the rebels rallied all classes to rise in revolt against the British. As support for the movement blossomed, Lucknow garrison troops crowned the son of their former king. People from all classes participated as the movement lashed out at symbols of British influence.

Most attackers limited their activity to localized areas and thus they did not spread or unify with other anti-British groups elsewhere in India. The rebellion was a multiclass movement, but leadership often fell to those of the lower orders who failed to expand their vision beynd a small locality. This, in conjunction with British views that the revolt had been carefully plotted out by a few devious leaders, turned the tide. British forces returned with a vengeance and crushed the rebels. Afterward, the British crown took control of India directly. Thus, this particular alternative vision for India faded, though the urge to create some alternative continued.

## QUESTIONS FOR CLASS DISCUSSION

1. What were some of the major characteristics of the antiimperialist prophetic movements?

2. What distinguished the nineteenth-century European "reactionaries," "liberals," and "radicals" from each other?

3. What were the major elements of Marx's understanding of history?

4. Why did insurgency movements become commonplace during the nineteenth century? How did tradition strengthen these movements? Why did they all ultimately fail?

5. What did the alternative visions of the nineteenth century seek to accomplish? What advantages did they offer the people that created them?

## MULTIPLE-CHOICE QUESTIONS

1. The "alternative" visions of the nineteenth century all sought to
   a. oppose authority and protect local community.
   b. overturn traditions.
   c. form imperialist empires.
   d. maintain exactly the same system with no changes.
   e. institute modernizing reform.

2. The Wahhabi Movement sought to institute pure Islam and challenge
   a. the Habsburg Empire.
   b. the Persian Empire.
   c. the Chinese Empire.
   d. the Ottoman Empire.
   e. the British Empire.

3. Allied to Wahhabi Movement leaders was the Najdian House of Saud of
   a. the Arabian Peninsula.
   b. Manchester, England.
   c. Delhi, India.
   d. Nanjing, China.
   e. Cairo, Egypt.

4. Which of the following did Shaka *not* use in his command of the Zulus?
   a. terror
   b. violence
   c. discipline
   d. mercy
   e. warfare

5. The Taiping Rebellion of China gained momentum from all *except* which of the following?
   a. pressures on the land due to population increases
   b. social instability from widespread opium use
   c. the government's loss of legitimacy due to its inability to manage foreign imperialism
   d. China's long tradition of peasant and religious rebellions
   e. government reforms aimed at relieving economic pressures by lowering taxes

6. Hong Xiuquan's Taiping society demonstrated all *but* which of the following?
   a. equality between the sexes
   b. Bible teachings
   c. common property
   d. restrictions on gambling
   e. free opium use

7. Which of the following best describes what reactionaries sought to accomplish?
   a. to jail all slow-thinking people
   b. to reverse democracy and secular influence
   c. to limit state power while expanding that of the individual
   d. to reconstruct society economically
   e. to destroy all government systems

8. Which of the following best describes what liberals sought to accomplish?
   a. to educate all slow-thinking people
   b. to reverse democracy and secular influence
   c. to limit state power while expanding that of the individual
   d. to reconstruct society economically
   e. to restore kings to the throne

9. Which of the following best describes what radicals sought to accomplish?
   a. to execute all slow-thinking people
   b. to reverse democracy and secular influence
   c. to limit individual power while expanding that of the state
   d. to reconstruct society economically and politically
   e. to reconstruct the great ancient empires of Europe

10. The materialist theory of history generated by Marx and Engels taught that
    a. what mattered was possessions.
    b. what mattered was how goods were produced and how that shaped social relations.
    c. what mattered was how often one went to work.
    d. what mattered was how often one could get out of work.
    e. what mattered was how much material was consumed by the economy.

11. Insurgents opposed to powerful colonizing nations generally preached a message that reflected all of the following *except*
    a. a combination of old ideas with some new ones.
    b. strong statements of universal love and toleration.
    c. idealized and glorified understandings of the past.
    d. strongly demonized portrayals of the colonizers.
    e. calls for solidarity among "oppressed" peoples of a particular region.

12. What did Tenskwatawa advise his followers to do to rid Indian lands of the white man?
    a. fight and destroy them
    b. pray
    c. return to the traditional Indian rites and lifestyle
    d. leave the Ohio Valley
    e. join the white man

13. Why did Mayan rebels stop their drive to rid the land of imperialists during the Caste War?
    a. Planting season came, so the Mayans went home.
    b. The Mayan warriors felt sorry for the white enemy.
    c. The white elites persuaded the Mayan peoples to stop.
    d. The Mayans refused to kill the Indian soldiers employed by the white elites.
    e. Mexico was fighting with the United States.

14. The Rebellion of 1857 in India was sparked by
    a. British construction of railways in India.
    b. the "greased cartridge" controversy.
    c. Russian advances in Siberia.
    d. British efforts to restore the Mughal emperor.
    e. heavy rains in the south of India.

15. The insurgencies discussed in this chapter were most commonly
    a. disbanded using gentle persuasion.
    b. dispersed after leaders were bought off.
    c. scattered after followers were persuaded to become Christian.
    d. destroyed with brute military force.
    e. completely ignored by the imperialist powers.

## MAP EXERCISE

Looking at a map of the globe, identify all the locations where "alternative" visions arose and what they might have all shared in common. Why were they called "alternative" visions?

## KEYWORDS

| | |
|---|---|
| Ghost Dance | Peterloo Massacre |
| The Battle at Wounded Knee | Peoples' Charter |
| *Muwahhidin* | Chartism |
| The Wahhabi Movement | Utopian Socialism |
| Fulani | phalanx |
| *jihad* | commune |
| *hijra* | Shawnees |
| Qadiriyya | Seven Years' War |
| Sufism | Prophet's Town |
| Sokoto Caliphate | War of 1812 |
| *Mfecane* | Caste War of the Yucatan |
| Zulu | Mayans |
| Opium Wars | Chan Santa Cruz |
| Taiping Rebellion | Tatish |
| Taiping Heavenly Kingdom | Tata Polin |
| (Heavenly Kingdom of | Balam Na |
| Great Peace) | Rebellion of 1857 |
| Restoration Period | East India Company |
| Pansophia | Kingdom of Awadh |
| Holy Russia | "greased cartridge" |
| Jacobins | controversy |
| liberals | sepoys |
| radicals | Bahadur Shah |
| Young Italy | *chapatis* |

## ANSWERS TO MULTIPLE-CHOICE QUESTIONS

| | | | |
|---|---|---|---|
| 1. | a | 9. | d |
| 2. | d | 10. | b |
| 3. | a | 11. | b |
| 4. | d | 12. | c |
| 5. | e | 13. | a |
| 6. | e | 14. | b |
| 7. | b | 15. | d |
| 8. | c | | |

# CHAPTER 17 | Nations and Empires, 1850–1914

## CHAPTER OBJECTIVES

- To describe various nation-building efforts in Europe and the Americas
- To explain the spread of imperialist empires around the globe and how industry, science, and technology helped enhance imperialist might
- To describe the reformist and expansionist impulses of Japan, Russia, and China as a result of a perceived imperialist threat

## CHAPTER OUTLINE, CHRONOLOGY, AND SUMMARY

As Cuban and Puerto Rican nationalists discovered, by the latter half of the nineteenth century, new world powers embracing the nation-state system and territorial expansion had begun to emerge. Using the ideals of popular sovereignty, capitalism, industrialization, and the new visions of social ordering that these nations championed, revolutionaries began to challenge the power of the old aristocratic elite.

## Nation-Building and Expansion

Nation-state advocates asserted that the globe was divided into peoples or nations of common heritage and territory that required a state. Often, however, it was the state that created the nation by imposing standardized laws, time, administration, language, etc., on a diverse population to create a common identity. The Americas, Japan, and parts of Europe provide the best examples. In Europe, states appeared as revolutionaries broke away from multinational empires unable to keep their lands intact.

Territorial expansion, however, complicated the needs of the nation-state by introducing a new "people" outside the people defined by the nation. Nevertheless, the alleged benefits were asserted to outweigh the costs. By century's end, nation-state competition for colonies led to a "scramble" for land that consumed the entire globe and led to goods and people crossing borders like never before.

## Expansion and Nation-Building in the Americas

In the Americas, elites moved to build strong nation-states based on inclusive government and territorial expansion. Expansion, however, did not involve colonization so much as conquest and incorporation of frontier territory into the nation-state itself.

### THE UNITED STATES

Despite distinct lines of fracture, Americans successfully carved out a strong nation-state. Territorial expansion provided a means of unifying the country as well as bringing prosperity to the white farmer. "Manifest Destiny" ideals also required, however, the suppression of Amerindians and conflict with Britain and Mexico. Despite the unity of territory, divisions over who constituted the "people" ultimately generated the Civil War, which itself ushered in the supremacy of the national government.

Economic growth exploded after the Civil War with new technology greatly accelerating agricultural and industrial output. Growth also led to social stratification that compounded tensions as overproduction in the 1890s led to unemployment and calls to restructure the American economic system. Loss of frontier and class unrest stimulated overseas expansion, which climaxed in the U.S. war with Spain and annexation of the Philippines. Although the United States had become a world power on ideals of equality, there was no common agreement on what form that equality should take.

## CANADA

Obtaining independence from England peacefully, Canadians quickly had to grapple with differences among themselves. Canada's French-speaking population wanted to preserve its cultural integrity without being absorbed into the English world. Anxious to preserve unity, the Canadian state used territorial expansion as a means of offering opportunity to Canadians. (Canada also thus kept its western territories from falling into the hands of the Americans.) The government encouraged the construction of westward railways and established treaties with the Native Americans. These changes strengthened the state, but the concept of nation among Canadians remained weak into the twentieth century.

## SPANISH AMERICA AND BRAZIL

In Spanish America and Brazil, expansion into the frontier went not to small farmers but to landed elites with huge plantation estates. Wealth and political influence thus remained limited to a few. Fear of rebellion led elites to jealously guard their economic dominance and political power by curbing the rights of the poor and nonpropertied. The nation-state thus excluded large segments of society from both the nation and the state. Brazilian elites suffered when slavery was banned but adapted and kept their plantations intact. Exclusive suffrage laws kept voting rights from the vast population of freed slaves while territorial expansion and railways created economic opportunities to keep the system afloat, at least until the rubber industry went bust.

Although nation-states generally sought to build economic prosperity and unity among citizens, some struggled to reach their ideals. All states in the Americas used territorial expansion to assure prosperity, but this also introduced new peoples who were not included in the nation.

## Consolidation of Nation-States in Europe

The failed revolutions of 1848 created bitter enemies to Europe's conservative monarchical elites. They also, however, strengthened the monarchies by aligning them with liberal revolutionaries who recoiled from radicalism. National competition justified uniformity within political constituencies and equated diversity with state weakness. While revolutionaries asserted that the state belonged to the "people," few could agree on exactly which people were to be included. Liberals, seeking state strength as well as economic opportunity, determined that the "people" did not include the working class, because workers threatened cherished bourgeois values. The union of conservative elites and middle-class liberals led to a nationalism that undercut the radical message.

## UNIFICATION IN GERMANY AND IN ITALY

German and Italian leaders seized on radical and liberal nationalist sentiment to form their respective nations. From nationalist movements arose unified states able to compete with the military and economic might of the great monarchical powers. Both Italy and Germany, however, emerged as aristocratic bureaucracies, not republics. Divisions continually hampered integration. Southern Italian elites resisted northern political objectives, and Germany struggled to integrate ethnic minorities through Germanization programs. Despite difficulties, Germany prospered economically and politically.

## CONTRADICTIONS OF THE NATION IN EUROPE

As suggested by the name, the Austro-Hungarian state suffered from fragmentation in the form of ethnic division. Slavs, Czechs, Poles, and others sought representation and voice in the new system. As various interests competed for influence, ethnic nationalist sentiment competed with the multinationalism of the state, leading to political paralysis. France and Britain also struggled with division, both class and national, as demonstrated by troubles with France's Socialist Commune and England's struggle with the Irish.

## Industry, Science, and Technology

Industry, science, and technology greatly enhanced the strength of the Western European, Japanese, and North American nation-states.

## NEW MATERIALS, TECHNOLOGIES AND BUSINESS PRACTICES

Changes in the late nineteenth century produced the second industrial revolution, which reordered ties between different parts of the globe. New technologies and materials, such as steel and electricity, greatly enhanced productivity, as did the wedding of science to technological development. Banks and joint stock companies made capital widely available, fueling the rise of huge companies that increased exports overseas.

## INTEGRATION OF THE WORLD ECONOMY

Profound appetites for cheap labor and natural materials, especially those unavailable in Europe such as rubber, led corporations to extend their influence overseas. Military, transportation, and communication technology favored European dominance by making the globe smaller and integrating the economies of nations. Scientific understanding expanded as scientists examined all parts of the globe. Darwin introduced ideas about the theory of evolution and concepts such as "survival of the fittest." Many came to believe these same principles applied to the human realm and justified Western expansion by claiming that Europeans were simply "fit" to expand and dominate other peoples. Social Darwinists also asserted that the poor suffered because they were unfit to do otherwise.

## Imperialism

The successes of imperialism convinced Europeans that they were indeed "fittest." By the end of the nineteenth century, the struggle to compete with other nation-states had driven Europeans to conquer all over the globe.

### INDIA AND THE IMPERIAL MODEL

Noting popular discontent with the Rebellion of 1857, the British moved to implement a system that capitalized on desires to make India a working colony. Ending East India Company rule, the British administration moved to modernize India with new infrastructure, irrigation, and public works. Agriculture flourished and contributed to British financial strength, although peasants earned diminished returns on their labor. British efforts to unify India laid the foundation for Indians to create a national identity, particularly when Indians were excluded from full citizenship in the British system.

### DUTCH COLONIAL RULE IN INDONESIA

The Dutch sought even more regimented control, setting prices and rents in Indonesia. Forced to grow export staples like coffee, the Indonesian peoples suffered from dropping food production. As starvation ensued, local peoples rebelled, prompting warfare and reform of the government. The Dutch gained economically, but the native people did not enjoy full status as citizens even in their own lands.

### COLONIZING AFRICA

The division of Africa into colonies took less than thirty-five years. British penetration and the discovery of gold and diamonds stimulated other European powers to rush for colonial holdings. To avoid conflict, Germany hosted a conference, the participants of which determined to recognize each other's acquisitions in Africa. European division of the continent divided tribes and threw diverse peoples together. Adventurers and missionaries contributed to European interest in Africa as British and German holdings expanded. King Leopold of Belgium carved out of the Congo his own personal state of terror and slaughter. African leaders either negotiated to reduce the loss of their land or fought, although most fought and were crushed. Only Ethiopia emerged strong enough to resist European expansion by playing the powers off one another and securing arms for its own army. Others fell victim to Europe's superior weaponry and tactics, or, like Samori Touré, were simply worn down.

### COLONIAL ADMINISTRATIONS

Colonial administrations often relied on military might and terror. Most European leaders sought to enrich themselves first and thus skimped by arming native supporters to protect European dominance. With time, European governments intervened to assure more civil administration by putting down revolts, seeking fiscal independence, and attracting missionaries, settlers, and merchants. New agricultural products contributed to economic independence of the colonies, although the producers again got little for their efforts. Mining also produced great profits but disrupted family life for tens of thousands of miners. European power in Africa, although appearing strong, depended on African-based armies and thus remained fragile.

### THE AMERICAN EMPIRE

Extending Manifest Destiny, seeking new markets, and offering to civilize the world, Americans also turned to empire building. Taking Cuba, Puerto Rico, and the Philippines, the United States disregarded earlier promises of freedom and instead produced new colonies. Like the European powers, the United States had formally entered the realm of imperialism by intervening in the affairs of other countries.

### IMPERIALISM AND CULTURE

Social Darwinist ideas combined with ideals of Europe's civilizing influence to justify imperialist expansion. The popularity of these ventures helped unify the people at home by lifting national pride and creating new images of national triumph. Motherhood was a highly regarded value, both in its ability to produce strong nationals and in the maternal regard Europeans held for their colonial charges. The adventurous European lad became a common image that pitted young men against the enemies of civilization—namely, Africans and Orientals.

## Japan, Russia, and China

Other powers also struggled to unify people and expand influence.

### JAPANESE TRANSFORMATION AND EXPANSION

Facing the unequal treaties imposed by American Commodore Matthew Perry, Japan determined to modernize and adapt. Led by the Meiji Emperor, reforms in education, the military, local administration, and so forth, quickly produced a strong national identity among Japanese. Economic transformation occurred even as the Meiji government fashioned a modern constitution. Great corporations, like Mitsubishi, dominated the Japanese economy and contributed to impressive growth rates.

Like other modernizing powers, Japan turned to territorial expansion. The Ryūkyūs were taken first, with ventures in Korea following shortly thereafter. Competition with China resulted in the Sino-Japanese War (1895) in which Japan won handily. For their efforts, the Japanese gained Taiwan and, later, the annexation of Korea. As in colonies elsewhere, the colonial masters exploited resources and introduced modernization, but only for their own benefit. Profit from the colonies reverted back to Meiji modernization programs.

RUSSIAN TRANSFORMATION AND EXPANSION

Expanding southwest and east, the Russians utilized the model of territorial integration employed in the Americas. Defeated in the Crimean War, Russian leaders determined to embark on a modernization program to ensure against similar fates in the future. Reforms affected all aspects of Russian life: peasant livelihood, military systems, education, industry, and so forth. Reforms also brought critics of the autocratic regime, however, and fragmented Russian society. Expansion helped redeem the regime by earning the respect of Russia's people. Conquest was followed by waves of settlers to increase Russia's influence and prevent Britain from expanding.

In East Asia, expansion into the Amur River basin brought Russians in contact with the Chinese. Deciding to concentrate its efforts in Asia, Russia sold Alaska to the United States and proceeded to construct the transcontinental railroad. Expansion helped unify Russians somewhat, but also added over a hundred new nationalities to the mix. Control came by centralized authority as Russia sought to assimilate these peoples. Ultimately, expansionism and requisite national defense stretched Russian resources even as Russia sought to keep its external enemies at bay.

CHINA UNDER PRESSURE

Unlike the Japanese or Russians, the Chinese did not view European expansion as a threat. Worried more about internal conflict, the Qing court repeatedly underestimated the power of European might. The Self-Strengthening Movement sought to arm China with Europe's superior weaponry, but did not produce the quality of experts or modernized equipment as first hoped. Chinese did expand into frontiers like Taiwan (before Japan took it away) and Xinjiang as population pressures rose, but they did not accompany expansion with modernization. Newspapers were one exception.

China's defeat in the Sino-Japanese War led many to call for widespread reforms. The reform movement, however, failed when the emperor's aunt arrested the young emperor and executed all reformers taken into custody. China's system remained too wedded to the traditional Confucian system to adequately respond to the challenges of Western-style modernity.

## QUESTIONS FOR CLASS DISCUSSION

1. How did colonialization occur in the New World? Why did it adopt the specific features and forms that it did?

2. Why did Europe's national movements compete so strongly with Europe's empires?

3. In what ways did industry, science, and technology give advantage to imperialist nations in their quest to build colonial empires?

4. How did imperialist powers justify their colonial expansion?

5. Why did Russia and Japan embark on expansionist quests of their own?

## MULTIPLE-CHOICE QUESTIONS

1. Institutions that help states reinforce strong feelings of nationalism among its people include all of the following *except*
   a. an education system.
   b. a national language.
   c. a unified system of laws.
   d. a belief that all people on the globe were one giant family.
   e. a national army.

2. What most contributed to the supremacy of the U.S. federal government over state governments?
   a. Manifest Destiny
   b. the Civil War
   c. economic growth
   d. the U.S. conquest of the Philippines
   e. the U.S. war with Spain

3. What was the Canadian government's attitude toward westerly expansion?
   a. It opposed westerly expansion because it did not want conflict with the native peoples.
   b. It refused to discourage westerly expansion but did not want to look too eager to seize the west.
   c. It actively promoted westerly expansion out of fear the United States might grab portions of it.
   d. It paid no attention to westerly expansion because it had other issues to worry about.
   e. There was no westerly expansion.

4. How did expansion in Spanish America and Brazil differ from that in the United States and Canada?
   a. The experiences were identical—land was taken from natives and given to newcomers.
   b. In the north, land was not taken but was purchased from the Indians.
   c. In the south, land was not taken but was purchased from the Indians.
   d. In the north, land went to small farmers. In the south, it went to huge plantation estates.
   e. No expansion occurred in the north or the south.

5. Which two European nations rose as newly unified nation-states in the late nineteenth century?
   a. France and Britain
   b. Portugal and Spain
   c. Poland and Russia
   d. Germany and Italy
   e. Greece and Israel

6. Which three nations boasted the greatest industrial output during the late 1800s and early 1900s?
   a. India, China, and Japan
   b. Mexico, Canada, and France
   c. Britain, Germany, and the United States
   d. South Korea, Singapore, and Indonesia
   e. Africa, Australia, and Greenland

7. Which of the following are good examples of the technological changes associated with the "second industrial revolution" of the late nineteenth century?
   a. steel and electricity
   b. wood and water
   c. iron and coal
   d. silicon and light
   e. lead and nuclear power

8. Social Darwinists taught that
   a. strong cultures were meant to dominate weak cultures.
   b. strong cultures were supposed to help and socialize with weaker cultures.
   c. weak cultures could eventually become strong.
   d. weak cultures needed to be sociable so strong cultures would not dominate them.
   e. strong cultures and weak cultures alike had a right to exist.

9. During the late 1800s, imperialism was encouraged by all *except* which of the following?
   a. beliefs that imperialism was lucrative and could make your nation wealthy
   b. rivalries between powerful nations seeking to gain an advantage
   c. Darwinist assertions that strong nations must expand
   d. technological supremacy that made conquest relatively easy
   e. notions that all peoples of the world, great and small, were created equal

10. Which European leader conquered the Congo of Africa and ruled it with blood and terror?
    a. King George of England
    b. King Leopold of Belgium
    c. King Ferdinand of Spain
    d. King Louis of France
    e. King Arthur of Camelot

11. European colonial administrations depended primarily on which of the following to preserve their power in Africa?
    a. large armies made up of African soldiers, which were trained and led by Europeans
    b. the sharing of profits with African peoples
    c. offers of modernization to the African peoples
    d. popular support at the polls
    e. the spread of European culture and religion among African peoples

12. The U.S. conquest of the Philippines led to
    a. the gradual incorporation of Filipinos into the "people" of the United States.
    b. the forced domination of Filipinos but little inclusion of them as U.S. citizens.
    c. the Philippine vote to join the United States as a state of the union.
    d. the expulsion of Russia from the Philippines as a former colonial master.
    e. great enthusiasm among Filipinos for a chance to immigrate to the United States.

13. After being opened by American Commodore Perry, Japan
    a. quickly fell into sub-slave status and economic ruin.
    b. quickly broke apart into warring states and political fragmentation.
    c. quickly adapted by implementing modernization programs and expanding its own borders.
    d. quickly fell victim to Chinese wars of expansion.
    e. quickly fell victim to British wars of expansion.

14. Russian expansion gained from urgent fears of
    a. outside threats from Japan, the Ottomans and Persians, and Europe.
    b. a new outbreak of Asian diseases.
    c. global warming.
    d. economic collapse if Siberia remained undeveloped.
    e. native insurgents opposed to the Russian ruling house.

15. One major obstacle to China's reform in the late nineteenth century was
    a. the emperor's conservative aunt.
    b. Japan's unwillingness to help China reform.
    c. U.S. efforts to keep China weak.
    d. China's tremendous lack of natural resources.
    e. repeated U.S. attempts to conquer China.

## MAP EXERCISE

Looking at a map of the globe, estimate what percentage of the world's land was conquered by imperialism during the years 1850 to 1914. How much was conquered between 1492 and 1914?

## KEYWORDS

Habsburg Empire
Ottoman Empire
Romanov Empire
Russification
Americans
Louisiana Purchase
Manifest Destiny
Civil War
Ku Klux Klan
Standard Oil
United States Steel
Populists
Greenbacks
dominion in the British
  Commonwealth
Royal Canadian Mounted
  Police (Mounties)
métis
"Order and Progress"

tappers
Manaus Opera House
Reich
Reichstag
the Compromise of 1867
Austro-Hungarian Empire
potato famine
Eiffel Tower
Suez Canal
"survival of the fittest"
Social Darwinism
Raj
"home charges"
Dutch East India Company
Peace of 1815
Afrikaners
Great Trek
"scramble for Africa"
Congo Independent State

*bula matari* (the breaker of
  rocks)
Maxim gun
Asantehene
Battle of Adwa
*Force Publique*
*mission civilisatrice*
native paramountcy
Spanish-American War
*Kinder, Küche, Kirche*
Tokugawa Shogunate

Meiji Emperor
Meiji Restoration
*zaibatsu*
Sino-Japanese War
Crimean War
Trans-Siberian Railroad
Treaty of Nanjing
Self-Strengthening
  Movement
*Shenbao*
Hundred Days' Reform

## ANSWERS TO MULTIPLE-CHOICE QUESTIONS

| | | |
|---|---|---|
| 1. d | 6. c | 11. a |
| 2. b | 7. a | 12. b |
| 3. c | 8. a | 13. c |
| 4. d | 9. e | 14. a |
| 5. d | 10. b | 15. a |

# CHAPTER 18 | An Unsettled World, 1890–1914

## CHAPTER OBJECTIVES

- To explain the rise of antiimperialist sentiment and the development of cultural tensions in Europe and North America
- To describe cultural "modernism" as a global historical phenomenon
- To illuminate the construction of various visions of "nation" and how "race" was used in these visions

## CHAPTER OUTLINE, CHRONOLOGY, AND SUMMARY

Violent suppression of rebellions, such as that following the Maji-Maji Revolt, cast shadows over Europe's imperialist enterprise. Discontent in Europe emerged alongside rebellion in the colonies, causing some to wonder if European dominance would last. Europeans composed almost a third of the world's population, commanded a higher percentage of its wealth, and shaped most major decisions. By the beginning of the twentieth century, economic, political, and cultural changes provided great opportunities but also tremendous anxiety.

### Progress, Upheaval, and Movement

Everywhere, radicals and reformers agitated for political and social change. Economic progress and stratification led many to condemn the division between rich and poor. Urbanization provided new roles for people as old roles were disrupted. Science contributed to "modernist" critiques of traditional worldviews, which in turn affected culture and the arts. In all, the identities of nations and people came to be more strongly redefined, eventually contributing to the devastation brought by World War I.

### People in Motion

Seeking better opportunities, land, and livelihoods, Europeans, Indians, and Chinese emigrated in extraordinary numbers. The number relocating to less distant locales also exploded. Cities, frontier, and precious commodities all attracted migrants. Motivation for movement ranged dramatically, but most planned impermanent moves in part due to the terrible risks involved. Before 1914, few restrictions on immigration existed because it was viewed as helping both the countries losing people and those gaining them. Cities swelled, leading to new developments in urban planning to improve conditions. Classes remained largely segregated. Many women found new options, but race, national identity, and mythic history were generally used to justify inequalities.

### Discontent with Imperialism

As imperialists relied more and more on harsh repression to maintain control over their colonial holdings, faith in the civilizing influence of Europe gave way to doubt and distress, especially as episodes of colonial rebellion increased.

UNREST IN AFRICA

Fierce uprisings in Africa particularly unsettled Europeans who struggled to understand why Africans would reject the fruits of modernity. Rebellions came at a steady pace, even after areas had been "pacified." The Afrikaner War, fought between two white states over the gold-laden Transvaal, introduced guerrilla warfare, concentration camps, and modern

50

reporting of the carnage. News of German genocidal policies was just as chilling. Apologists tried to soften the horror by portraying Africans as innocents and other imperialists as the cause of problems.

### THE BOXER UPRISING IN CHINA

After facing a humiliating defeat in the Sino-Japanese War, China turned to meet expanding Western influence as the powers carved out "spheres of influence." Although anxious to carry out reform, the Chinese emperor found powerful opponents. Conservative and anti-European to an extreme, these opponents sought a chance to destroy imperialism.

Incidents involving missionaries offered imperialists a pretense to make demands on the Chinese government, fostering resentment at all levels of society. From the bottom strata of Chinese society emerged the Boxers—martial arts groups that aimed at ridding China of Christians once and for all. Poverty and natural disaster stimulated the growth of the Boxers, including the female Red Lanterns. Magical tokens and chants gave both groups confidence to act.

Unable to check the growth of the Boxers, the conservative court encouraged them to attack foreigners instead of Chinese Christians. Violence led to bloodshed before a multinational force arrived to crush the Boxers and place punishing exactions on the court. The Qing, somewhat humbled, moved to reform the government but only succeeded in alienating its own populace. Although the Boxers failed, they demonstrated how unpopular the foreign presence had become and what a loyal populist movement could accomplish.

## Worldwide Insecurities

In Europe and North America, news of distant problems could be explained away, but political and economic signs of disruption at home could not.

### IMPERIAL RIVALRIES COME HOME

Expansion and economic competition led to rising military competition across Europe and the rest of the globe. The consolidations of Italy and Germany disrupted the old balance of power and stimulated a massive arms race.

### FINANCIAL, INDUSTRIAL, AND TECHNOLOGICAL INSECURITIES

The dominance of huge capitalist firms over small entrepreneurs also gave cause for concern. By the end of the nineteenth century, economies were stuck in a cycle of boom and bust that ruined small operations and favored larger companies that concentrated economic power in the hands of a few. Free market competition dropped as huge industrial magnates came to control more and more of the economy, leading to widening disparities. Organizing to protect themselves, farmers formed cooperatives, while the big industrialists organized cartels. Some called for greater government intervention. Financial crises between 1890 and 1907 led the U.S. Congress to ratify the Federal Reserve Act to better manage financial problems.

Economic crises also created ripple effects in Canada, Mexico, and other states relying on American capital. Industrialization spread in places like Russia, but lagged elsewhere, creating a gap in industrial capacity. Factories and railways brought opportunity, but also breaks with the past and, according to some, the reduction of humans to machine-like existences.

### THE "WOMAN QUESTION"

The changing roles of women in a modern world produced another source of anxiety. Job and educational opportunities expanded, allowing women to play a more active role in public life. As women found other occupations, birthrates dropped, thus providing more resources for the children that families raised.

Political rights came slowly due to male resistance. Radical views stiffened male, and even female, reluctance to support dramatic change. Imperialists liked to claim they assisted women in their plight by attacking suppressing traditions such as footbinding. Colonized women, however, noted that colonization just as often added to their struggles, for example, by taking the men out of the house to work in a factory or mine and leaving the women to labor by themselves on the farm, lose traditional ownership rights, or fall behind in educational opportunities.

### CLASS CONFLICT IN A NEW KEY

Closed political systems, loss of confidence in capitalism, and rising inequalities led many radicals to reject the status quo and organize workers in an effort to agitate for change. Regimes successfully expanded the electorate in hopes of deflating support for the radicals, yet many outbursts still occurred among other groups not so favored.

In the United States, laborers organized in increasingly greater numbers, leading to strikes such as the Pullman Strike. Although that strike collapsed, disruption from below, as seen in Russia after the Russo-Japanese War, did succeed for a brief time. The Mexican Revolution, in which impoverished people rose up to topple the regime of General Porfirio Díaz and sustain a populist political culture, signified to many what the lower classes could do when sufficiently motivated. Many more bottom-up revolutions, however, did not fare as well.

Unable to suppress agitation, some regimes instituted welfare changes to steal thunder from the Socialists. Government regulation and oversight led to the correction of abuses and greater protection of workers and consumers. Reformers cleaned up urban vice, built parks, attacked corruption, and intervened to help the poor, sick, and aged, creating precedent for the modern welfare state.

## Cultural Modernism

Intellectuals, artists, and scientists also struggled with the changes of a new age. "Modernism" and its ideas flourished as thinkers sought to reconcile new understandings with older views, explore the cultural expressions of non-Europeans and the lower classes, and challenge the certainty that all things European were best.

### POPULAR CULTURE COMES OF AGE

By the turn of the century, education and urbanization had created vast numbers of literate consumers engaging in new forms of popular culture that spanned sports, theater, and art. The "yellow press" appealed to the tastes of the lower classes and provided the proletariat with their own sense of identity even as they drew inspiration from a broader range of cultural experiences.

### EUROPE'S CULTURAL MODERNISM

In Europe, attempts to understand social problems, spearheaded by thinkers such as Freud, Durkheim, and Le Bon, led to the gradual formation of the social sciences. Artists questioned the so-called progress of Europe's modernization, turning to the "primitivism" of Oceania and Africa for inspiration. Classical and Christian art themes gave way to art depicting dreams, machine aesthetics, and antibourgeois forms. Scientists accelerated the collapse of European confidence by concluding that the natural world operated on probabilities, not certainties, ensuring that man would never fully know its mysteries. The belief in rationality also came under fire. Nietzsche and Freud asserted that rational thinking could not motivate or explain the deeper elements of human nature.

### CULTURAL MODERNISM IN CHINA

In China, debate centered on modernism took a slightly different turn. Chinese writers began exploring new vistas—self, technology, and sexuality. Numerous visions of modernity, drawing from Chinese tradition and Western mores, competed for the attention of thinking Chinese. Urban centers, with their new wealth, education, and exposure to the West, hosted most activity. Art and literature explored new visions of the future. While many thinking Chinese valued Western science, finding a way to integrate it into Chinese culture presented a problem. What was the role of traditional Chinese beliefs in a modern world?

## Rethinking Race and Reimagining Nations

Even as people moved from place to place, their identities became more rigidly defined. Race became a key for determining inclusion or exclusion from a nation and in fixing a cultural identity. Racial hierarchies and biological determinism was used to justify imperialism as well as exclusion of certain people from the mainstream of society. Racial interpretations of global affairs ranged from fear of "impure" racial influence to anticolonial pride in racial difference. Most, however, agreed on racial purity and appealed to powerful arguments for panethnic communities.

### NATION AND RACE IN NORTH AMERICA AND EUROPE

America greeted the new century with pride in its technological prowess and fear of the loss of natural resources. Wide-open frontiers had vanished along with the bison. Confessing that markets could not protect the land, Teddy Roosevelt moved to create the National Forest Service to manage public lands and provide future generations a chance to build character by "roughing" it.

Concerns about racial division also characterized the early twentieth century. "Jim Crow" laws and Exclusion Acts protected whites from blacks and Asians. Nonwhite immigrants, including those from U.S. territories, raised concerns among whites and led to tighter immigration restrictions. Europeans struggled with the same concerns, particularly as anticolonialism spread through Africa and elsewhere. Whites worried that mixing with nonwhites weakened the nation's blood stock and deprived the country of its virility. Racial purity, in short, was seen as the solution to national problems.

### RACE-MIXING AND THE PROBLEM OF NATIONHOOD IN LATIN AMERICA

In Latin America, races were arranged in a hierarchy that placed Iberian whites at the top, followed by creoles, indigenous peoples, and Africans. The hierarchy did not stick, however, largely because immigrants complicated the picture. Some asserted that mixed racial compositions would only lead to degeneration and that white immigration was the only solution. Others, however, sought to build legacies to the past that combined European and indigenous Aztec roots. In contrast to those condemning multiracial nations, these Latin American thinkers asserted that multiracial integration is what gave their nations vitality and strength.

### SUN YAT-SEN AND THE MAKING OF A CHINESE NATION

Chinese thinkers also asserted that a strictly pro-Western view was too narrow. Claiming Han Chinese superiority, they reinvented the past to save it from modernization and westernization. Selective borrowing and adaptation thus became common among nationalist thinkers. In seeking to build a strong Han Chinese nation, Sun Yat-sen attacked the Manchu court of China while calling for democratization, land reform, and a modern economy. Banned from China, Sun found support among the hundreds of thousands of Chinese living and studying abroad. As the Qing weakened, his message grew stronger and, in 1911, most Chinese sided with his revolutionary supporters. The new republic aimed originally to combine the "five races" of China. Modeling his views on concepts learned in the West, however, Sun eventually sought to replace a multiracial empire with a single-race nation.

## NATIONALISM AND INVENTED TRADITIONS IN INDIA

British rule in India engendered among Indians a concept of "India" that had not existed before. Anticolonialism, therefore, began to employ nationalistic language and was headed by Western-trained intellectuals. Newspapers contributed to the spread of new identities. Organizing the Indian National Congress in 1885, Indian nationalists argued with the British government for better representation.

Nationalism in India was based on culture and sought to find a non-Western modernism that fit India's specific conditions. To define what was meant by the term "Indian," intellectuals created a national culture and legacy from the myriad of artistic, historical, linguistic, and cultural possibilities before them. Within this redefinition, Hindu cultural icons dominated while Muslim traditions were largely neglected.

Radical agitators of the Swadeshi Movement sought violent means to oust the British and greatly broadened the nationalists' base of popular support. Successes signaled that the British had lost control. Other ethnic and religious groups also organized, using the same approach employed by Hindu nationalists, except that they placed themselves at the core of "Indian" civilization. Most sought political advancement of their own groups. By the late nineteenth century, anticolonial movements in India had adopted some variety of nationalism.

## THE PAN MOVEMENTS

Although also fixated on race, the pan movements sought a different ordering of society. They wanted borders realigned so races across the globe could be united. The pan-Islam movement of Jamal al-Din al-Afghani begged Islamic nations to put differences aside and unite under one banner. Few followed the call. Most Muslims saw little commonality with Afghani's vision and felt more secure in building their own nation-states.

Pan-Germanism, partly a reaction to pan-Slavism and Jewish immigration from Russia, sought to unite all Germanic peoples and strengthen them against Catholic influence, division (between Germany and Austria), and the Jews. Like the others, pan-Slavs also engaged in radical activities designed to weaken national boundaries that kept Slavs apart. Indeed, it was one such agitator that assassinated the heir to the Habsburg throne and ushered in the Great War. The First World War did destroy the multinational empires that pannationalists so detested, but did not create the panvision they sought.

## QUESTIONS FOR CLASS DISCUSSION

1. Why did colonial peoples lose confidence that colonialization was "best" for them?

2. Why did the Boxer Uprising in China fail? What did it need to succeed?

3. What were some of the tensions that Europeans and North Americans struggled with during the two decades spanning the turn of the century? How did these issues reflect concerns that were beginning to appear in the colonies?

4. How did modernism represent a loss of confidence in older traditions and beliefs?

5. Why did race come to be viewed as a primary element of nationalist visions across the globe?

## MULTIPLE-CHOICE QUESTIONS

1. Problems and anxieties associated with the years leading up to 1914 include all *but* which of the following?
   a. discontent among the colonized with imperialist intervention
   b  frustration with the inequalities associated with the global economy
   c. irritation with the seedy and inhumane aspects of big city life
   d. anger at social injustices facing poor workers and peasants
   e. fear of nuclear war and the end of humanity

2. Massive migrations before 1914 were fueled by all *but* which of the following?
   a. economic opportunity in the form of jobs and land
   b. a chance to get wealthy via new discoveries of precious metals
   c. famine and social turmoil
   d. missionary desires to gain converts
   e. overwhelming desires to stay put and make due as best as possible

3. The Boer War was fought between
   a. two white states in Africa.
   b. two black states in Africa.
   c. the British and the Rhodesians.
   d. the Russians and the United States.
   e. the British and the Swedes.

4. The Boxers in China sought
   a. to destroy organized bandit groups in China.
   b. to destroy foreigners and their influence in China.
   c. to attack the Qing government.
   d. to disrupt trade so they could gain control over it.
   e. to disrupt political negotiations between Britain and China.

5. African and Chinese uprisings against imperialist intrusion before 1914 taught most Europeans that
   a. imperialism was an evil enterprise and should be abandoned.
   b. imperialism should be made less imposing and threatening.
   c. other cultures were inferior.
   d. other cultures were superior.
   e. all of humanity shared common desires, goals, and objectives.

6. How did the rise of huge industrial cartels affect free market competition?
   a. competition greatly increased
   b. competition moderately increased
   c. no effect
   d. competition moderately decreased
   e. competition greatly decreased

7. Industrialization, as reflected in the spread of railways and factories, led to frustrations in all the following ways *except*
   a. it destroyed towns that happened to be left off railway lines.
   b. it polluted the air, water, and land.
   c. it unnaturally forced workers and animals to conform to the tempo of machines.
   d. it produced great quantities of affordable goods and made them available to most people.
   e. it forced communities to abandon their ties to the past.

8. Which of the following best describes the impact imperialism had on colonized women?
   a. It reduced women to virtual slaves.
   b. It released women from some burdens, like foot-binding, but produced others.
   c. It greatly enhanced their status and well-being.
   d. It reinforced traditional mechanisms that kept women in their traditional roles.
   e. It generally had no impact on women at all.

9. At the turn of the nineteenth century, which of the following did *not* contribute to uprisings from below?
   a. closed political systems
   b. loss of confidence in capitalism
   c. rising inequalities

   d. dissatisfaction among groups who felt out of favor in their respective countries
   e. the stock market crash

10. Which of the following was *not* a way that governments tried to weaken the power of radical movements?
    a. They passed laws banning brutal abuses of workers and offering them some protection.
    b. They instituted some welfare reforms to steal the thunder of the radicals.
    c. They attacked corruption in their own government system.
    d. They suppressed radical organizations.
    e. They ushered radicals into the government to help steer government policy.

11. "Cultural modernism"
    a. confirmed belief that all good things come from Europe.
    b. corroborated belief that rational thinking and science will eventually discover all truth.
    c. taught colonized peoples that Europeans had a higher civilization.
    d. taught Europeans that imperialism was justified.
    e. cast doubt on traditional faith in rationality and European dominance.

12. "Jim Crow" laws in the United States sought
    a. to segregate blacks and whites.
    b. to join blacks and whites together in tight-knit communities.
    c. to ban the sale of alcohol.
    d. to prevent Asian immigrants from coming to the United States.
    e. to give blacks a chance to get out of poverty.

13. Discussions of race before 1914 often asserted all *but* which of the following?
    a. Biological ancestry impacted culture.
    b. Genetic predispositions of a group could affect social problems such as alcoholism.
    c. Cultural identity needed to consider race.
    d. The concept of race was an artificial and man-made construction.
    e. The whole world could be ranked by race.

14. Which of the following criteria was most important to Sun Yat-sen as he sought to define the "Chinese" nation?
    a. race
    b. language
    c. culture
    d. economics
    e. politics

15. Which of the following was most important to Indian nationalists seeking to define "India" as a separate nation?
    a. race
    b. language
    c. culture
    d. economics
    e. politics

## MAP EXERCISE

Looking at a map of the globe, try to identify what the world would have looked like if the major "panmovement" activists had all been able to accomplish their dreams.

## KEYWORDS

*maji*
Maji-Maji Revolt
Mahdi
Afrikaners
Afrikaner War
*uitlanders*
Sino-Japanese War
Open Door Policy
Boxer Uprising
Taiping Rebellion
Red Lanterns
Boxer Protocol
Federal Reserve Act

"Haussmannization"
syndicalism
socialism
anarchism
Labour Party
German Social Democratic
    Party
American Railway Union
Pullman Strike
Russo-Japanese War
Meat Inspection Act
Progressive Era
modernism

"art for art's sake"
"yellow press"
*calaveras*
"talking cures"
primitivism
Bohemian
*Pierre Lunaire*
modernity
Shanghai School
race

Swadeshi Movement
1882 Exclusion Act
"Jim Crow" laws
Indian National Congress
Indian National Muslim
    League
Zionism
pan-Islamism
pan-Germanism
pan-Slavism

## ANSWERS TO MULTIPLE-CHOICE QUESTIONS

1. e
2. e
3. a
4. b
5. c
6. e
7. d
8. b

9. e
10. e
11. e
12. a
13. d
14. a
15. c

## CHAPTER 19

# Of Masses and Visions of the Modern, 1910–1939

## CHAPTER OBJECTIVES

- To describe the Great War and the postwar order
- To explain the rise of mass-based culture, production, and consumption
- To describe the different visions of mass-based modernity driving postwar political movements

## CHAPTER OUTLINE, CHRONOLOGY, AND SUMMARY

World War I was truly a global conflict, spanning from Europe to Turkey to Africa. In Africa, like elsewhere, people became disillusioned with European colonialism and harbored notions of freedom and self-determination. The war forced liberal regimes to rethink mass society and find solutions to economic problems. By the eve of World War II, the strength of autocratic regimes called into question the value of building nations on liberal ideas of limited government and individual initiative.

## Economic and Political Modernities

In the 1920s and 1930s, many visions of modernity competed. Common to most of these visions, however, was the predominance of mass production, mass consumption, and mass culture. The Great Depression called these into question, however, leading to the emergence of three new visions of modernity: liberalism, authoritarianism, and anticolonialism. Liberalism, which wed capitalism and democracy, suffered during the Great Depression as economies collapsed. While many considered alternatives, liberalism survived by

granting more power to the state. Authoritarian regimes exalted the state by subordinating the individual and rejecting democracy in favor of authoritarian control and government distribution of "national" resources. Anticolonialism rejected liberalism, calling it a mechanism of imperialism, and sought the expulsion of foreign powers from native lands. Modernity, after all, first required independence.

## The Great War

The Great War destroyed European claims to civilized superiority and demonstrated how much states relied on their people. Rivalries and balance-of-power shifts caused the war, and alliances determined who fought on what side. The assassination of Archduke Francis Ferdinand of Austria was the trigger.

### THE FIGHTING

Excitement about the war quickly wore off as defensive technologies overwhelmed offensive capabilities and the war ground to a deadlocked struggle of attrition. High death rates pushed up recruitment, eventually bringing women into the war as part of auxiliary units and as factory workers. The number of casualties soared, especially as civilians became military targets and influenza spread across continents. The war stretched to all corners of the globe and led to revolt among colonized peoples and Europeans alike. Russia's Romanov Empire fell to Lenin's Bolsheviks. U.S. intervention, which tipped the balance in favor of the Allies, combined with fears that Socialism was spreading in Germany to break the Central Power alliance apart. The Prussian Empire became a republic while the Habsburg and Ottoman Empires fragmented into smaller states.

THE PEACE SETTLEMENT AND THE IMPACT OF THE WAR

The Versailles Peace Conference blamed Germany for the war and exacted stiff reparations. Former Ottoman territories fell to France and Britain. U.S. President Woodrow Wilson hoped to create a world order that would bring about peace and self-determination for all people, but he found little support among allies abroad or in Congress at home. Women came out of the war claiming new privileges. Losing their new factory jobs to demobilized soldiers, they turned their attention to gaining more influence in the political and social arena.

## Mass Culture

Propaganda, which combined music, theater, and newspapers, stimulated the rise of mass culture after the war by constructing an audience for film and radio. Mass culture differed from elite culture in that it appealed to working-class and middle-class tastes. It also relied on new technology that allowed it to reach citizens all across the nation. Mass culture thus became much more closely aligned with the nation than elite culture.

Radio reached millions of homes, providing entertainment for even uneducated families while creating a sense of intimacy between radio personality and listener. It also served political interests, particularly in authoritarian states where it promoted the state agenda, although it was also used against dictatorships. Film also promoted certain agendas, either to entertain or propagandize a population. Capitalists employed radio and film for their own purposes—the advertisement of their products—and succeeded in reaching even international markets.

## Mass Production and Mass Consumption

Rising to meet the enormous demands of the Great War, industry streamlined and perfected the production of material goods. After the war, industry could produce consumer goods in much greater quantities and for less, making possible a culture of mass consumption. Rising as an economic power after World War I, the United States became the model of mass consumption and unprecedented prosperity.

MASS PRODUCTION OF THE AUTOMOBILE

Henry Ford's mass production of the automobile exemplified the ties between mass production and consumption better than any other development. Popular demand inspired Ford to create the assembly line, which drove production up and prices down. Road building, mining, glass manufacturing, and other attendant industries ensured that huge numbers of American workers had jobs thanks to the automobile industry. Paying his workers double the going rate for industrial labor, Ford also expanded the market for his automobiles.

THE GREAT DEPRESSION

Overproduction of staple goods led to falling prices and rural worker dissatisfaction with their lot relative to that of urban worker. When the American stock market collapsed, financial institutions all across the globe closed their doors. Governments instituted protectionist measures shutting down most international trade. Manufacturers fired millions of workers before folding. So great was the impact, that the viability of markets began to be rethought. Many assumed that only state intervention could prevent such disasters. Thus was laid the foundation for the welfare state. Indeed, many regimes gave up on free-market capitalism entirely.

## Mass Politics: Competing Visions of Becoming Modern

For many people, World War I destroyed the liberal dream of technological progress, free markets, and government by the educated few. Sacrificing for their nations, those on the lower tiers of society now clamored for a greater share of the economic and political pie. Socialism began to spread while revolution threatened colonial empires. Many liberal regimes collapsed in the wake of the Great Depression. Others lost faith in liberalism and turned to authoritarian solutions. By the 1930s, liberal states looked weak and dictatorships appeared strong.

LIBERAL CAPITALISM UNDER PRESSURE

Europeans sensed that modernity had only corrupted their societies and looked elsewhere for sources of strength. Some found it in cultures not yet tainted by westernization. Others turned to more authoritarian development of the state, a natural extension of bureaucracies bloated during World War I.

*British and French Responses to Economic Crises* Pressures from the working class and ex-soldiers forced British and French elites to adjust their systems to better accommodate popular demands. Strikes were commonplace as coalition governments sought to steer their respective countries out of economic crisis. Radicalism thrived in France and successfully secured working-class reforms.

*The American New Deal* In the United States, the Great Depression came at a time when conservatism was sweeping the land. Republican leaders focused on capitalism and markets free of government interference, rather than poor farmers or African Americans who were left behind. The Great Depression, however, forcibly changed the tone of American politics. Once in power, Roosevelt instituted the New Deal to provide a safety net for the most destitute of Americans. While unable to end the Depression or produce growth, Roosevelt's welfare programs and state manipulation of the economy managed to save capitalism by holding authoritarianism at bay.

## AUTHORITARIANISM AND MASS MOBILIZATION

Dictatorships promised to transcend the decadence of liberal democracies and create orderly, dynamic societies under the rule of charismatic leaders. All claimed to enjoy the support of the people and assured them that the benefits of modernity could be created while avoiding its downsides. Many believed these claims.

*The Soviet Union* Taking power in 1917, the Bolsheviks began immediately shoring up their power to defend against attacks from multinational expeditions and White Russian enemies. Success greatly strengthened expansionist tendencies. Stalin succeeded Lenin and moved to construct Socialism, which he defined as anticapitalism. Violence sought to rout signatures of capitalism and led to the organization of giant collective farms. Many peasants protested and were deported to remote areas. Crop failures led to some privatization but no decline of state dominance. In cities, the Five-Year Plan aimed to surpass Western industrial productivity and build up Socialism. Huge projects symbolized Soviet greatness. The system, however, grew despotic. Purges routinely eliminated "enemies" among the Soviet elites while terror extended down to all levels of Soviet society.

*Italian Fascism* Suffering from popular agitation, postwar Italy appeared to be heading toward Socialism. Mussolini's Fascists promised to eliminate the Socialist threat in favor of a populist movement that won support from wealthy and poor alike. Marching on Rome with his black-shirt shock troops, Mussolini used intimidation to gain the position of prime minister. Using his influence to move Italy to one-party rule, Mussolini's government served as a model for seizing power and deflecting Socialist revolution.

*German Nazism* Sent to observe a new nationalist group, Adolf Hitler soon rose to command it. Hotly nationalistic, the Nazis combined anticapitalism, anti-Semitism, and repudiation of the Versailles Agreement. Arrested for trying to seize power, Hitler went to jail and wrote *Mein Kampf*. Turning to a new approach, the Nazis began to build support among those suffering under terrible inflation. Success at the polls eventually ushered Hitler into power as chancellor. Fanning fears of a Communist conspiracy, he expanded his power to that of dictator. Crushing dissent and attacking Jews, he asserted the ideas of a pure race in Germany. A restored economy and pride in Germany won Hitler support. Pronouncing the rise of the Third Reich, Hitler set his sights on global conquest.

*Militarist Japan* Japan prospered during World War I and moved from a debtor nation to a creditor nation. Economic development astounded observers. Liberal democratic reforms were adopted, expanding the ranks of voters. At the same time, however, fear of Communism justified repressive measures against leftist organizations. Under Emperor Hirohito's rule, economic difficulties produced unemployment, prompting military leaders to ignore policies of the civilian government. Violence, at the hand of patriotic societies and young military officers, intimidated government leaders. Expansionism could not be restrained as the military began to conquer parts of China without the approval of Japan's government.

*Common Features* Each of these regimes shared certain common features. All rejected parliamentary rule. All espoused state involvement in controlling the economy. All employed mass organizations and focused on rallying the youth. All but one (Japan) employed large-scale welfare programs and policy. All asserted traditional roles for women out of the public realm, while struggling to enforce their ideal. All employed terror against their own citizens, colonial subjects, and foreigners. All successfully mobilized popular support. All also generated admirers and imitators elsewhere.

## THE HYBRID NATURE OF LATIN AMERICAN CORPORATISM

Latin American states employed elements from democracy and authoritarianism to solve their problems. Falling exports during World War I stimulated radical movements. The Depression brought state intervention into Latin American economies. Corporatist alliances, such as that of Vargas in Brazil, united elites and mass organizations to help maintain elite positions by building support through popular policies and paternal concern for the masses.

## ANTICOLONIAL VISIONS OF MODERN LIFE

In the colonies, what to do about imperialism overshadowed questions regarding the relative benefits of democracy or authoritarianism. After World War I, Britain had more colonies than ever. While extending self-rule privileges to white-dominated territories, nonwhite areas were denied such privileges. To African and Asian intelligentsia, throwing off the colonial yoke first required some form of nationalism. Some nationalists believed in constructing democracy while others turned to Fascism or Communism. They also drew from their traditional culture for inspiration regarding the new modern order they sought to create. Ultimately, how long imperialism had dominated and to what degree it dominated greatly impacted the outcome of the anticolonial movement.

*African Stirrings* Still in the process of constructing their movements, African anticolonialists wondered whether European offers of modernity were sincere or merely a ruse to extract more. Largely excluded from the political arena, Africans began testing the limits of French and British rule with protests, strikes, and boycotts. Europeanized African elites, however, often sided with the imperialists rather than the protesters.

*Imagining an Indian Nation* Already quite articulate by the early twentieth century, Indian anticolonialism provided a model for other movements to emulate. Excluded from politics and angered by British atrocities, Gandhi transformed the Indian National Congress into a mass movement dedicated to Indian self-determination through nonviolent means. The Salt March attracted millions and won international acclaim. While Nehru gave support, Gandhi's methods did not appeal to radicals or to Muslims. Rebuffed in elections, Jinnah moved to build the Muslim League into its own nation, separate from India and in contrast to the more Hindu-flavored Indian National Congress. Nationalist goals overshadowed all others, including attempts by women to gain political rights. Nevertheless, by the time Britain began to open the political sphere, Indian unity had split.

*Chinese Nationalism* Like the others, Chinese nationalists sought to oust imperialists in order to build a strong, modern state. Following the Qing collapse in 1911, power fell from Sun Yat-sen to military strongman Yuan Shikai, before his death fragmented political power. Student protests prompted Sun to revive his Guomindang party and to cooperate with the Russians to defeat imperialism. Chiang Kai-shek, who succeeded Sun, again unified China before breaking with the Russians and building a modern culture based on Confucianism and fascism.

*Peasant Populism in China: The White Wolf* The Guomindang did not, however, implement any changes in the countryside. There, a grassroots movement arose largely unchallenged. White Wolf earned popular support by plaguing the rich while giving to the poor. White Wolf's success demonstrated the power of working with peasants and the limited ability of the Guomindang to reach China's rural masses.

*A Post-Imperial Turkish Nation* No anticolonial and modernizing movement succeeded in the 1920s and 1930s like that of Turkey. Fearful that Ottoman collapse would reduce Turkey to a colony, Turkish nationalists rallied to create a modern nation-state. War and negotiation opened the way for modernization and a democratic government based on secular law rather than Muslim conventions. State involvement in the economy, racial theories, and secret police emerged to ensure success.

*The Muslim Brotherhood in Egypt* In Egypt, nationalism surged when Zaghlul was forbidden to present the Egyptian case at the Versailles Peace Conference. British efforts to pacify popular anger only exacerbated tensions, leading to some Egyptian independence in 1922, but under British watch. During the Great Depression, Egypt's liberal system fell to the Muslim Brotherhood, which denounced liberalism and Communism while calling for a return to Islam.

## QUESTIONS FOR CLASS DISCUSSION

1. What were some of the short- and long-term impacts of the Great War?

2. What were the political implications of mass culture?

3. How did the development of mass production and mass consumption shape economic and political history?

4. Why did liberalism decline in popularity after the Great War and during the Great Depression? What might have caused people to support authoritarian regimes?

5. Why did anticolonialism become particularly widespread after the Great War and during the Great Depression?

## MULTIPLE-CHOICE QUESTIONS

1. During the 1930s, the three visions competing for the right to define what "modernity" meant included the
   a. liberal, authoritarian, and anticolonial programs.
   b. Chinese, Russian, and U.S. programs.
   c. Buddhist, Catholic, and Muslim programs.
   d. the European, Asian, and African programs.
   e. the expansive, contemplative, and explorative programs.

2. The Great War
   a. created admiration among colonized people for Europe's great military might.
   b. destroyed European claims to civilized superiority.
   c. generated great funding drives among colonized peoples to help rebuild Europe.
   d. had no effect on the colonized peoples of the world.
   e. remained a mystery to the colonized peoples of the world.

3. Fighting during the Great War
   a. demonstrated great grace and beauty as armies sought to outmaneuver each other.
   b. remained limited to European soil.
   c. involved only European soldiers.
   d. showed little movement as it soon became mired in a defensive deadlock.
   e. remained relatively light with few casualties.

4. The Russian Revolution eventually ushered who into power?
   a. the tsar
   b. the Kaiser
   c. the Bolsheviks
   d. the peasants
   e. the democrats

5. Originally, Woodrow Wilson's idealist vision of the post-Great War era included all *but* which of the following?
   a. strict restrictions on Britain to prevent it from again threatening world peace
   b. the League of Nations
   c. self-determination for colonized peoples
   d. the blessing of liberal freedoms for all mankind
   e. collective security to prevent rogue states from threatening peace

6. The rise of radio and film helped authoritarian regimes by
   a. providing free advertising of authoritarian products.
   b. offering new and effective mechanisms for mass propaganda.
   c. providing the state with a new form of revenue.
   d. giving the government new access to news around the globe.
   e. producing a new type of investigative reporter that could criticize the government.

7. Henry Ford's great contribution to mass productivity was
   a. the light bulb.
   b. the Model T.
   c. assembly-line manufacturing.
   d. the radio.
   e. paid holidays for workers.

8. The Great Depression caused many to accept
   a. claims that the market needed government intervention to keep it in balance.
   b. the assertion that capitalism is best.
   c. views that government had no business interfering with business.
   d. the opinion that a declining market was still better than no market.
   e. that some people are just unlucky and there is nothing to be done about it.

9. Which of the following best describes how various European people living through the Great Depression thought about government systems?
   a. All forms of government are bad.
   b. Liberalism is the best form of government.
   c. Liberalism was in decline and authoritarianism was better.
   d. Liberalism is good but so is authoritarianism.
   e. Authoritarianism is evil.

10. The New Deal sought to
    a. provide a safety net for America's unemployed and destitute.
    b. declare war on Germany.
    c. restructure the American government system along Fascist lines.
    d. make a pact with the Japanese.
    e. destroy Socialism in the United States through military action.

11. The Russians, under Stalin, defined Socialism to emphasize all of the following *except*
    a. opposition to capitalism.
    b. soviets (councils) of worker and peasant deputies.
    c. the importance of serving the interests of the rich.
    d. government involvement in economic planning.
    e. restrictions on private ownership and trade.

12. Hitler eventually became chancellor of Germany
    a. by seizing it in a coup.
    b. by intimidating his enemies with assassination.
    c. by entering into secret negotiations with the Japanese.
    d. by repeatedly winning at the polls.
    e. by taking control of the military.

13. Authoritarian regimes shared all *but* which of the following features?
    a. some measure of state control over the economy
    b. particular attention to the organization of youth
    c. terror against their own citizens
    d. mobilization of popular support
    e. careful attention to the electorate and election campaigns

14. Anticolonial movements shared all but *which* of the following features?
    a. some form of nationalism
    b. inspiration from traditional cultures as a means of shaping nationalism
    c. dissatisfaction among nationalists with their own exclusion from power
    d. a steady commitment to democracy
    e. efforts to harness antiimperialist sentiment

15. Gandhi's nonviolent revolution utilized all of the following *except*
    a. seizing the moral high ground by rejecting violence.
    b. high profile but benign acts of resistance that attracted the press and popular attention.
    c. boycotts of British goods and strikes in British factories.
    d. massive support among Indians swayed by his vision.
    e. heavy reliance on British sympathizers who acted as spokespersons for the movement.

## MAP EXERCISE

Looking at a map of the globe, identify what new countries arose from the rubble of the Romanov, Prussian, Ottoman, and Habsburg Empires respectively.

## KEYWORDS

Great War
modernity
mass production
mass consumption
Model T
Great Depression
liberal
authoritarian
anti-colonial
Central Powers
Triple Entente
Allies
Western Front
"no man's land"
"Africa for the Africans"
Romanov regime
Duma
February Revolution
Bolsheviks
Eastern Front
Versailles Conference
League of Nations
Nazis
assembly line

Black Tuesday
Keynesian Revolution
liberalism
Socialism
Weimar Republic
Nazi Germany
Munitions Ministry
Progressive Era
"Jim Crow" laws
"New Negro Movement"
"Harlem Renaissance"
New Deal
Federal Deposit Insurance
    Corporation
National Recovery
    Administration
Works Progress
    Administration
Social Security Act
Whites
Reds
New Economic Policy
kulaks
class warfare

Five-Year Plan
Gulag
black shirts
*Il Duce*
National Socialist German
    Workers' Party (National-
    Sozialisten, or Nazis)
Beer Hall Putsch
brown shirts
Third Reich
Meiji Emperor
Manchukuo
Shinto
*zaibatsu*

British Commonwealth of
    Nations
Indian National Congress
*satyagraha*
the Salt March
Muslim League
Versailles Treaty
Russian Revolution
White Wolf
Suez Canal
Wafd
Young Egypt
Muslim Brotherhood

## ANSWERS TO MULTIPLE-CHOICE QUESTIONS

1. a
2. b
3. d
4. c
5. a
6. b
7. c
8. a

9. c
10. a
11. c
12. d
13. e
14. d
15. e

# CHAPTER 20 | The Three-World Order, 1940–1975

## CHAPTER OBJECTIVES

- To outline the general features of World War II and how it precipitated the cold war
- To describe the cold war's "three-world" order and the process of decolonization
- To explain various tensions in each of the "three worlds"

## CHAPTER OUTLINE, CHRONOLOGY, AND SUMMARY

At Yalta, even before the end of World War II, the United States, Russia, and Britain harbored very different visions of the coming world order. World War II destroyed Europe's dominance, leading to a three-world system. Locked in the cold-war struggle were the First World—the United States and allies—and the Second World—the Soviet Union. The Third World included virtually everyone else.

### Competing Blocs

Confident in the universal applicability of their respective ideologies, the United States and the Soviet Union moved to expand their spheres of influence and defend against each other with great stockpiles of nuclear weapons. It was in the Third World, however, that most hostility broke out as anticolonial nationalists sought independence. Freedom, however, did not automatically bring economic strength as new states sought to build new political orders for themselves. Democracy and material goods gave Americans confidence but could not overshadow racism and unpopular wars. The Soviet reliance on crushing repression undermined its social welfare policies. By the early 1970s, rising economic might in Asia and radicalism elsewhere challenged the dominant First and Second Worlds.

## World War II and Its Aftermath

German and Japanese desires to expand brought them into conflict with France, Britain, the Soviet Union, and the United States, among others. The total devastation of World War II ended all claims of superior civilization among Europeans and stimulated anticolonial movements to press for independence.

### THE WAR IN EUROPE

The Nazis conquered most of Western Europe with their *blitzkrieg* attacks. In subdued territories, puppet regimes sent millions of foreign laborers to work in German factories while genocidal policies sent Jews and gypsies to concentration camps. Soviet armies stopped Hitler's advance at Stalingrad in 1942 and began driving him westward, gaining momentum when the United States and Britain landed at Normandy on June 6, 1944. Germany surrendered on May 7, 1945.

Enormous destruction and death were left in the wake of the war. Six million Jews, a full two-thirds of Europe's Jewish population, had been decimated in the concentration camps.

### THE PACIFIC WAR

Anxious to create a colonial empire in Asia, Japan occupied Manchuria in 1931 and then attacked China in 1937. Unable to force China's surrender, the Japanese imperial army brutalized the Chinese, particularly those in Nanjing. Determined to take the oil and rubber resources of Southeast Asia, Japan moved into Indochina but aggravated the United States in the nearby Philippines. Surprise attacks at Pearl Harbor aimed to weaken the Americans for a time and give Japan time to complete the conquest of Asia. Vast territories were taken, including the Philippines, before the Americans came roaring back. Japanese abuses did not win the support of the Asian peoples they conquered, and soon the United States had put Japan on the defensive. Despite overwhelming failures, the Japanese refused to surrender until President Harry Truman ordered the atomic bombing of Hiroshima and Nagasaki. After surrendering, Japan was then occupied by American forces.

## The Beginning of the Cold War

Much of Europe was left in ruins at the end of the war. A massive rebuilding program would be necessary to restore order and services.

### REBUILDING EUROPE

With their countries in ruins, many Europeans looked to Communist leaders, who had distinguished themselves fighting Fascism, for direction in forming powerful egalitarian societies. Alarmed that Communism was spreading, U.S. policymakers identified Stalin as a threat and moved to "contain" Communism by preventing its spread. As a symbol of contention, the western portion of Berlin was walled up and Germany was split between the democratic West and the communist East. The Truman Doctrine and the Marshall Plan offered economic and military aid to wrecked nations as a means of weakening calls for Communism. The United States also helped form NATO, an alliance of Western nations designed to oppose the Soviets. Moscow responded with the Warsaw Pact.

### THE NUCLEAR AGE

Both sides built up their arsenals of nuclear weapons. By 1960, each had the power to destroy the world and thus moved cautiously to avoid full-scale confrontations with the other. In Asia, where no clear line separated one side from the other, wars broke out regularly, beginning with the Chinese civil war and the Korean War. To help in Asian wars, the United States pressured Japan to become an active ally in the region in exchange for economic help.

## Decolonization

After colonial empires collapsed during World War II, colonized peoples were determined to forge their own nations. Decolonization followed three patterns: civil war, negotiated independence, and incomplete decolonization.

### THE CHINESE REVOLUTION

China's case represents the first pattern. Chinese Communists, working in the countryside since 1927, sought to build a new society strong enough to resist enemies like the Japanese. The Japanese invasion of 1937 gave Mao Zedong's rural Communist movement a chance to grow behind enemy lines and win popular support among the peasants by organizing them as guerrilla fighters. Embracing all Chinese groups, in-cluding women, the Communist movement swelled, growing from about 40,000 in 1937 to over 100 million by 1945.

After the Japanese surrender, fighting resumed between Mao's Communists and Chiang Kai-shek's Nationalist Government. Losing first popular support and then the civil war in 1949, Chiang retreated to Taiwan while Mao moved to build Communism in China and to provide inspiration to other Communist movements around the globe.

### NEGOTIATED INDEPENDENCE IN INDIA AND AFRICA

Independence came with little bloodshed in the British territories of India and Africa. Seeing the writing on the wall, the British simply withdrew.

*India* British talk of departure left Indian nationalists in disagreement as to the direction India should take: Gandhi's nonmodern, self-governing village communities or Nehru's modern nation-state. Congress leaders convinced the British to hand power to them, a notion the British preferred over looming radical uprisings. At the same time, however, Hindu-Muslim unity fragmented. The new nation was largely defined in terms of Hindu culture, with which the Muslims shared little in common. Anxious to please, the British divided the colony into two states: Hindu India and Muslim Pakistan. Gaining independence in August 1947, celebration turned to horror as a million Hindus and Muslims killed one another. Gandhi stopped the violence long enough for 12 million people to migrate north or south, depending on their religious preference, but was himself shot dead six months later. Afterward, Nehru took inspiration from both the United States and the Soviet Union to modernize India.

*Africa for Africans* In Africa, rapid decolonization occurred through the 1950s and early 1960s. Anticolonialist nationalists learned how to build powerful movements based on the poor, ex-servicemen, and educated elites. Pressured by the United States and the Soviet Union, Britain gave up its African colonies one by one. Charismatic leaders heading populist movements became the new administrators. French territories followed a similar course although France strongly resisted losing its colonies at first. Once it was clear that the French electorate had no desire to grant full privileges to overseas peoples, the French government moved to turn most of its colonies loose, with the exception of Algeria. Hoping to build on traditional African community values, many African leaders sought a new modernity—a type of African socialism that rejected cold individualism in favor of social justice and equality. Léopold Sédar Senghor's "Negritude," for example, envisioned a society that celebrated African values and community while accepting the better elements of French culture.

### VIOLENT AND INCOMPLETE DECOLONIZATIONS

In some colonies, the presence of white colonists greatly complicated the transfer of power to new African colonial leaders. In others, like Vietnam, efforts to find a "third way" were thwarted by superpower requirements that colonies remain true to capitalist or Communist lines.

*Palestine, Israel, and Egypt* During World War I, the British Balfour Declaration promised Jews a homeland in Palestine while also offering the Palestinians a state of their own. Anti-Semitism in Europe fueled Jewish immigration even as the British tried to limit it out of fear of provoking the Palestinians. In 1947, Britain handed the problem over to the United Nations, which separated Palestine into Jewish and Palestinian halves. Jews organized quickly as neighboring Arab nations moved to drive the Jews "into the sea," and successfully defeated the threat. Israel extended its territory, producing more than one million refugees living in camps. In Egypt, the Free Officers Movement under Nasser toppled the regime of King Faruq, redistributed elite lands, dissolved parliament, and turned on the Communists. Israeli forces, with British and French support, tried to take the Suez Canal from Nasser but were forced to withdraw, brightening Nasser's reputation as a symbol of pan-Arab nationalism.

*The Algerian War of Independence* French reluctance to grant Algerian independence stemmed largely from the powerful lobby of the *colons*: white French settlers who dominated Algeria's political and economic spheres. As anticolonial nationalism spread after World War II, France responded with military suppression. The nationalist Front de Libération Nationale responded with its own violence in 1954 and a vicious, bloody war of eight years ensued. Most French believed the *colon* argument that Algeria was part of France and supported the war until a *colon* insurrection brought Charles de Gaulle to power. Sick of the conflict, de Gaulle ended the war.

*Eastern and Southern Africa* In Kenya, the Mau Mau Uprising against white rule forced Britain to fly in troops before ultimately granting independence in 1963. In Portuguese colonies and Southern Rhodesia, war lasted much longer. Women played key roles. South African settlers maintained a firm grip through extreme racial segregation called apartheid. Nelson Mandela of the African National Congress first urged nonviolent resistance and later violent attacks against the white regime, but struggled as long as the United States supported South Africa as a bulwark against Communism.

*Vietnam* Finding their road to political influence blocked by French colonialists, young educated Vietnamese nationalists like Ho Chi Minh began agitating for independence in the 1920s. Learning of communism and agrarian revolution while abroad, Ho established the Viet Minh among Vietnam's peasantry. When France returned to reclaim Vietnam from the Japanese after World War II, Ho sought U.S. support but found none and had to defeat the French on his own. At the Geneva Peace Accords, following the French defeat in 1954, Vietnam was divided into a Communist north and a U.S.-controlled puppet south. The north determined to conquer the south while the United States moved to brace against the spread of Communism. Despite U.S. efforts, the south eventually fell to Ho's forces.

## Three Worlds

With decolonization creating new independent states, the superpowers positioned themselves to offer either democracy and capitalist economic growth or egalitarianism and rapid modernization respectively. Choosing to go their own way, many states struggled to modernize even as cold-war competition found its way into Third World politics.

### THE FIRST WORLD

The First World—Western Europe, North America, and Japan—built liberal versions of modernity but also found it convenient to align with Third World dictators in an effort to defeat Communism.

*Western Europe* U.S. economic support helped Western Europe recover from World War II devastation in remarkable ways. Agriculture and industry boomed, allowing for stable social and political systems resistant to Communist propaganda. Preservation of some Nazi elements in Germany ensured that Communism struggled in the West.

*The United States* During the 1950s, economic prosperity and a strong sense of faith in the country led to rising birthrates and national pride. At the same time, however, widespread and manipulated fear of Communist infiltration led to hardcore anti-Communist foreign policy and increasing arms expenditures. Eager to secure for minority groups the same right to prosperity enjoyed by whites, the Civil Rights Movement used nonviolence to demand (and eventually get) desegregation. The U.S. model thus combined liberal capitalism and increasing rights for all.

*The Japanese "Miracle"* Shattered by World War II, Japan embarked on a reconstruction program that impressed everyone. U.S. military protection kept Japan's military budgets small. American technology, investment, and markets, meanwhile, stimulated economic development and allowed Japan to produce one of the world's most powerful economies. In addition to U.S. help, the Japanese government orchestrated much of the success.

### THE SECOND WORLD

Determined to avoid future invasions from the West, the Soviets conquered Eastern Europe to serve as a buffer zone. Many supported the Soviet system as an effective alternative to capitalism's inherent problems. Soviet education, for example, excelled. Pride in the Soviet victory in World War II combined with skewed information on life in the First World to give citizens the impression that Soviet people enjoyed a living standard far superior to anyone else. As news of the outside trickled into Soviet-bloc nations, many still believed the Soviet system to be more just.

The Soviet system, however, relied on brutality and suppression. Millions suffered in the Gulag system simply because the government dared not trust them. Unrest led Khruschev to secretly denounce Stalin, signaling a wave of political and economic experimentation in Eastern European states anxious to loosen the tight grip of Moscow. Revolts in Hungary and Poland, although gaining small concessions, were crushed as a sign to all that Moscow still dominated. Intellectuals, youths, and workers clamored for more changes but were brutally squelched.

The Soviet Union's educational system, which trained many from the Third World, produced gifted scientists who eventually launched Sputnik in 1957. To many Soviet leaders, this advancement signaled that the Soviets were destined to surpass the First World.

### THE THIRD WORLD

Having ousted the imperialists, many Third World nations believed they could now create humane versions of modernity different from the systems of the First and Second Worlds. Eager to build democracy and rapid economic growth without materialism or oppression, Third World leaders plunged ahead.

*Limits to Autonomy* Maintaining a "third way" proved difficult for Third World states. The World Bank and the International Monetary Fund provided economic assistance, but also encroached on state autonomy. Multinational corporations, eager for profit, competed with native banks and remitted profits to First World stockholders. Politically, Third World leaders found themselves drawn into alliance arrangements, hosting U.S. or Soviet military bases, while also trying to build up their own military forces. Far from accomplishing their visions of a "third way," many Third World nations fell to dictatorships willing to play the superpowers off against each other for arms and assistance.

*Third World Revolutionaries and Radicals* Other attempts to find a "third way" led to radical views of social change, as represented by the writings of Frantz Fanon. In China, Maoist radical visions led to the Great Leap Forward, which killed some 20 million, and the destructive excesses of the Cultural Revolution. In Latin America, dreams of empowering the poor and reducing the influence of multinational corporations led radicals to violent confrontations with U.S. interests. Cuban failures to improve the lot of the working poor opened the door to radicals like Fidel Castro, who eventually instituted radical reform. Abortive U.S. efforts to dislodge Castro drove him into the arms of the Soviets and precipitated the Cuban Missile Crisis. Fearful of Communist spread into the Western Hemisphere, the United States initiated aid programs that taught the virtue of democracy while also expanding anti-insurgency forces to combat rising revolutionary movements. As anti-Communist concern rose, the United States found itself supporting violently repressive military regimes that liquidated huge segments of their own populations.

## Tensions in the Three-World Order

Radicalism did not succeed but did expose rifts and vulnerabilities within the First and Second Worlds.

### TENSIONS IN THE FIRST WORLD

National crises during the 1960s shattered the confidence, assurance, and unity Americans enjoyed during the 1950s. This occurred in spite of the fact that prosperity, rights, and opportunities expanded to groups formerly neglected. Race riots and violence marked a new course in the direction of the Civil Rights Movement. Women and minorities struggled for greater equality and empowerment. Intellectuals began to question the values of American society and then condemn them as the anti–Vietnam War Movement gained momentum.

### TENSIONS IN WORLD COMMUNISM

Fractures in Soviet unity appeared in 1948, when Yugoslavia wrested autonomy from Moscow, and in 1956, when Poland and Hungary attempted to do the same. The "Prague Spring" of 1968 did not succeed in its objectives but gained some concessions. Moscow eventually allowed some variation as pressure grew. The greatest crack in the Communist bloc, however, came when Chinese-Soviet relations broke down in 1960. Presenting peasant-led revolution as an alternative to proletariat-led revolution, the Chinese moved to supplant the Soviets as the head Communist state, precipitating a crisis in relations.

### TENSIONS IN THE THIRD WORLD

Never unified, the Third World labored to create cohesion. Collaboration rarely offered much. In the early 1970s, for example, the Organization of Petroleum Exporting Countries (OPEC) raised oil prices, precipitating an oil crisis as a means of pressuring Israel's allies. OPEC leaders, however, soon found themselves backpedaling when oil production in other newly discovered areas drove prices down and raised competition. Oil revenues also often profited First World banks or the multinational corporations in charge of refining and distributing oil. Some states, like Taiwan and South Korea, did break away from cycles of poverty. Here, however, success came from disciplined state regulation, education, help for new industry, and laws that kept multinational firms from destroying native industry.

## QUESTIONS FOR CLASS DISCUSSION

1. What is the "three-world order" and what were the major characteristics of each of the three worlds?

2. How did the United States aim to ensure Communism could not spread into Western Europe?

3. Why was the cold war accompanied by massive decolonization across the globe?

4. How did the end of World War II lead to the development of cold-war rivalries?

5. What tensions developed in each of the three worlds?

## MULTIPLE-CHOICE QUESTIONS

1. In general terms, both the United States and the Soviet Union believed *what* about their respective ideologies of liberal capitalism and Communism?
   a. that both views were good
   b. that both views had advantages and disadvantages
   c. that their own view had universal applicability, but the opposite view did not
   d. that their own view had universal applicability, and so did the other
   e. that neither view was suitable for humanity

2. What was the impact of World War II on European world dominance?
   a. It expanded European influence on the world.
   b. It contributed to the sharp decline of European influence on the world.
   c. It added a military dimension to Europe's already strong influence.
   d. It softened Europe's influence by fostering sympathy from other nations.
   e. It had no impact on Europe's influence on the world.

3. Which country was the first to turn Hitler's armies back?
   a. the Soviet Union
   b. Britain
   c. France
   d. Japan
   e. the United States

4. Japan's Greater East Asian Co-Prosperity Sphere struggled for all of the following reasons *except*
   a. Japanese racism against other Asians.
   b. Japanese brutality against other Asians.
   c. forced labor inflicted on other Asians.
   d. the pillaging of Asia's natural resources.
   e. Japanese promises to protect Asia from European imperialism.

5. The Truman Doctrine and the Marshall Plan aimed to
   a. ensure Japan would never again rise to become a military power in the Pacific.
   b. ensure Germany would never again threaten the world.
   c. ensure that the Soviet Union would never again threaten the globe.
   d. rebuild Europe's shattered economies so as to prevent the spread of Communism.
   e. rebuild the great American cities destroyed during World War II.

6. In Asia, where no line distinguished the democratic from the Communist states, wars broke out regularly. Which represent Asian wars that sought to stop the spread of Communist forces?
   a. the Korean War and Chinese civil war
   b. the Pacific War against Japan
   c. the Crimean War and Boer War
   d. the Sino-Japanese War of 1895
   e. the Russo-Japanese War of 1905

7. Mao Zedong's revolution succeeded largely because of all *but* which of the following?
   a. It implemented a rent reduction campaign for the peasants.
   b. It attracted nationalistic Chinese by waging a guerrilla campaign against Japanese invaders.
   c. It successfully employed propaganda geared for the common man.
   d. It targeted China's millions of peasants in the countryside instead of city dwellers.
   e. It collaborated with the Japanese and therefore was admired by peace-loving Chinese.

8. During the mid-1940s, India's nationalist movement split along which lines?
   a. ethnic lines
   b. religious lines
   c. linguistic lines
   d. geographical lines
   e. ideological lines

9. Upon gaining independence, many African leaders moved to
   a. build a modernity based on African culture.
   b. follow in the pattern of the Soviet Union.
   c. reject modernity and turn again to traditional culture.
   d. repudiate European culture and establish authoritarian regimes.
   e. adopt U.S. culture and politics as the norm.

10. British efforts notwithstanding, Palestine broke into fierce fighting between
    a. Palestinians and Arabs.
    b. Arab states and Israelis.
    c. the British and the Jews.
    d. Jews and Israelis.
    e. Arab states and the British.

11. Attempting to keep part of their colonial empire intact, the French fought bloody wars in
    a. Pakistan and India.
    b. China and Japan.
    c. Vietnam and Algeria.
    d. Rhodesia and South Africa.
    e. Egypt and Greece.

12. The "three worlds" constituting the cold-war era included all *but* which of the following?
    a. the First World or the United States and its European allies
    b. the Second World or the Soviet Union
    c. the Third World or all remaining decolonized nations
    d. efforts by the First and Second Worlds to win support from among the Third World nations
    e. efforts by the Third World to band together and militarily defeat the First and Second Worlds

13. Advantages of the Second World system included
    a. economic prosperity and increasing political rights.
    b. high levels of education and pride in the superiority of the system.
    c. strict control of information about the outside.
    d. brutal suppression of rebellion or dissent.
    e. international peace.

14. Mao Zedong's attempt to find a "third" way to modernity led to
    a. disastrous consequences that included mass starvation and social chaos.
    b. international prestige as long-term peace was finally restored to China.
    c. a great revival of China's economy.
    d. economic struggles but political stability.
    e. social successes and a few economic disappointments.

15. Which of the following does *not* represent one of the stresses in the First World?
    a. the Civil Rights Movement
    b. the Women's Movement
    c. the Anti–Vietnam War Movement
    d. Prague Spring
    e. race riots like those in the Watts area of Los Angeles

## MAP EXERCISE

Looking at a map of the globe, try to determine how geography might have contributed to India, Uzbekistan, and Japan belonging to the Third, Second, and First "worlds" respectively.

## KEYWORDS

Yalta Accords
First World
Second World
Third World
*blitzkrieg*
total war
*Luftwaffe*
S.S. (*Schutzstaffel*)
Auschwitz-Birkenau
Rape of Nanjing
Pearl Harbor
Tripartite Pact
Greater East Asian Co-Prosperity Sphere
"Asia for Asians"
Hiroshima
Nagasaki
Berlin Airlift
cold war
Federal Republic of Germany
German Democratic Republic
Berlin Wall
Truman Doctrine
North Atlantic Treaty Organization (NATO)
Warsaw Pact
Long March
Muslim League
Indian National Congress Party
Negritude
Zionists
Balfour Declaration
Free Officers Movement
Muslim Brotherhood
*colons* (settlers)
Front de Libération Nationale (FLN)

Kikuyu peoples
Mau Mau Uprising
apartheid
Group Areas Act
African National Congress (ANC)
Sharpeville Massacre
Viet Minh
Dien Bien Phu
Geneva Peace Conference
Viet Cong
Marshall Plan
baby boom
McCarthyism
National Association for the Advancement of Colored People (NAACP)
*tiers monde*
International Monetary Fund
World Bank
multinational corporations
SEATO
Baghdad Pact
Great Leap Forward
Great Proletarian Cultural Revolution
Red Guards
lost generation
Bay of Pigs
Alliance for Progress
Civil Rights Act
Voting Rights Act
"War on Poverty"
Black Panthers
Prague Spring
Organization of Petroleum Exporting Countries (OPEC)

## ANSWERS TO MULTIPLE-CHOICE QUESTIONS

| | | |
|---|---|---|
| 1. c | 6. a | 11. c |
| 2. b | 7. e | 12. e |
| 3. a | 8. b | 13. b |
| 4. e | 9. a | 14. a |
| 5. d | 10. b | 15. d |

# CHAPTER 21 | Globalization, 1970–2000

## CHAPTER OBJECTIVES

- To explain how the cold-war order gradually fell apart and how the obstacles to globalization were removed
- To identify various themes that define globalization today

## CHAPTER OUTLINE, CHRONOLOGY, AND SUMMARY

Today, more than ever, people, ideas, and things flow from one end of the world to the other. Ironically, while this phenomenon leads to diversification in one sense, as in Los Angeles, it also destroys diversity, as in the Amazon. Globalization has led to greater integration, but not equality. While some live the jet-set life, others battle to lift themselves out of poverty.

### Global Integration

Large political empires no longer drive change as in the past. With the fall of the three-world order, the open marketplace has appeared as a new interpretative paradigm. U.S. success has driven the globe in this direction, even as global cultures have redefined America. Also significant is the rise of transnational forces that have begun to affect the sovereign autonomy of nation-states. Education, economic prosperity, and political rights are expanding. Nevertheless, many still remain behind.

### Removing Obstacles to Globalization

As the three-world order crumbled, Second World options disintegrated leaving new ties to integrate the world.

#### ENDING THE COLD WAR

Cold-war hostilities greatly limited global exchange. Countries caught between the superpowers fell into chaos and war. The arms race led to enormous expenditures for weaponry that eventually bankrupted the Soviet Union and greatly raised U.S. debt. Economic challenges from outside their respective blocs and dissatisfaction from within eroded confidence. The Soviet bloc collapsed, revealing terrible shortages, lagging health care, and political lies. Gorbechev's efforts to reform the Soviet system undermined party control. It fell to Yeltsin to dismantle and privatize the vast Soviet system. Some states ceased to exist, such as East Germany. Others broke apart, such as Yugoslavia. For the majority, the breakup of the Soviet Union meant political and economic stagnation. Unable to absorb subtle technological changes, like the computer, in an information age meant that Communism could not sustain itself.

#### AFRICA AND THE END OF WHITE RULE

In the 1970s, few remnants of Africa's colonial experience continued to exist. The collapse of the Portuguese colonies ended all formal imperialist holdings, but some states continued to be dominated by white governments. When Rhodesia's white government buckled in 1979, South Africa's white leaders remained alone. In 1994, due to the failure of increasingly harsh measures against Nelson Mandela's African National Congress and fears of becoming even more of a pariah nation, South Africa's de Klerk organized free elections that swept white leaders out of power. Despite progress, most African states struggled to build their economies, to avoid falling too deep into cold war political rivalries, and to integrate various peoples within their states. Ethnic and local rivalries, however, beset such efforts, ensuring that neither peace nor stability could be guaranteed even after the end of the cold war.

### Unleashing Globalization

As obstacles to international integration dissolved, most states moved to stimulate "agents" of globalization, thus increasing contact but also widening inequities.

FINANCE AND TRADE

Pulling back from formal management of money, state leaders turned to policy that called for unrestricted, deregulated markets and profits rather than the welfare-oriented Keynesian approach. This made it easier for investors to transact business in the international financial sector. In the 1980s, Latin American nations, defaulting on IMF loans, widely opened domestic markets and initiated a boom in international finance which other countries followed. The Internet has allowed rapid movement of money.

Globalization has stimulated commercial interdependence as goods move around the globe. Trade has also shifted the division of labor as manufacturing spreads internationally and economic growth accelerates in places like Asia. Fearing competition, regional open-trade blocs such as NAFTA and the European Union have arisen. As changes occur, new goods have risen in importance, including services, computers, and pharmaceuticals. Information-based production has risen dramatically in wealthy nations while knowledge remains scarce in poorer nations.

MIGRATION

The movement of people has also increased integration as individuals and families leave poor countries to seek opportunities in wealthier ones. Ironically, migrants frequently follow the tracks of vacating imperialist powers. Even as corporations locate their factories in poorer nations, laborers there often prefer migration and the lowest wages in richer nations. International migration has been accompanied by regional and national migration from poor rural areas to urban centers, as in Nigeria. Migration is often viewed as temporary, particularly since it is difficult to integrate into European or Japanese society. Nevertheless, labor shortages often require these temporary migrant workers, who, establishing homes, become targets of exclusion and violence.

The United States has had less trouble integrating migrants coming from places like Mexico or Asia, and migration has transformed the ethnic composition of cities, particularly Los Angeles. As the number of migrant workers has increased, nations have had to grapple with relative integration and the ethnic makeup of political communities. While most migrants move voluntarily, many are still forced to move as a result of violence. Africa hosts the largest concentration of such migrants.

CULTURE

While American culture's popularity and spread is largely responsible for the rise of a global entertainment culture, it takes its cues increasingly from other parts of the world. Thus, on a global scale there is less diversity, but from the perspective of an individual with technological access there is opportunity for much more.

*New Media*  Cassettes and CDs, television, films, and even international cable networks have helped distribute culture around the globe. Sports have became an international industry, as evidenced by Michael Jordan's popularity and the impressive support of international sporting events like the World Cup.

*Global Culture*  Migration has allowed cultures to spill into new areas and take root or generate completely new genres. Often music or TV serials, for example, have become tied to youth or ethnic cultures trying to express dissatisfaction with the political status quo. Governments do not ignore these challenges and sometimes seek to resist "Americanization." At the same time, American culture has expanded to embrace other non-American performers.

*Local Culture*  Local cultural developments do not merely imitate global cultural norms, but they have often created expressions based on local or national cultural icons that have opened the way for black, female, and homosexual performers. Globalization has led to an increasingly homogenized world culture, yet has also stimulated local cultures that have become increasingly diverse.

COMMUNICATIONS

Advanced communications in the form of telecommunications, computers, and the World Wide Web have greatly increased the trend toward globalization. New opportunities for wealth creation over international boundaries have produced some of the world's richest people. Indian, Mexican, and Taiwanese firms produce computers and educate fleets of computer programmers. As communication opportunities expand, the gap between rich and poor has become increasingly determined by who can get online and who cannot. In short, globalization has led to integration, but also to wider economic disparities.

## Characteristics of the New Global Order

Globalization is changing the world. Expanding populations require greater agricultural and industrial productivity. Families are changing as are sources of social status. Material goods have become widely available but are not necessarily equitably distributed.

THE DEMOGRAPHY OF GLOBALIZATION

Declining mortality rates have boosted the world's population dramatically but at faster rates in Asia, Africa, and Latin America. Wealthier nations and the poorest nations show slower growth rates or declining rates. China's burgeoning growth rates led the government to adopt a "one-child policy." In wealthier nations, declining birthrates came as a matter of choice and lifestyle.

*Families*  The definition of family has become fluid, with divorces and out-of-wedlock births increasing.

*Aging* People live longer, creating older populations. Lower fertility rates have allowed the percentages of older citizens to rise, increasing the burden on society's yuonger generations as they try to support an expanding aged population. In societies that have no welfare programs, this creates dire circumstances.

*Health* In rich, modernized cities, epidemics have been held in check. Developing nations hosting urban squalor, however, still have trouble containing disease. The spread of AIDS has changed personal behavior and has led to a variety of expensive treatments unavailable in poorer nations where education has not been readily available.

*Education* In some areas like India, more men are better educated, while women still lag behind, often laboring under severe poverty. In the United States, women secure more than half of all college degrees. In China, education has made great strides but still has far to go in rural areas, particularly for women.

*Work* Women have entered the workplace in greater numbers but have yet to reach parity with men in their competition for top positions. Child care continues to divide the time of women. Working women in Canada and Australia needing child-care services often employ others who frequently end up being women from Jamaica or the Philippines with children of their own.

*Feminism* Feminist calls for changes in the status and condition of women went global in the 1970s. Seeking equal pay and opportunity, global feminism fights discrimination that keeps women in positions of subordination. In 1995, Beijing hosted the Fourth World Conference on Women to produce "a platform for action" on policies affecting women.

PRODUCTION AND CONSUMPTION
IN THE GLOBAL ECONOMY

Production and consumption have also changed considerably. How to feed a global population has been the predominant challenge.

*Agricultural Production* Chemistry and biology have accelerated agricultural production, but more so in America and Asia than elsewhere, where opening new land by destroying rain forests is cheaper. In Africa, agriculture simply has not kept up due to political constraints, lack of incentives, and poor markets for goods. Starvation, therefore, became common during the 1980s.

*Natural Resources* Americans produce much, but they consume great quantities of water, energy, and fossil fuels. In 1991, these consumption needs led to the Gulf War.

*Environment* Pollution has become a problem of global proportions. Many polluters have merely moved to poorer nations, thus shifting the onus. Pollution in poorer nations is often the price paid for economic development and payment of international loans. As pollution problems rise, national leaders find it increasingly difficult to reach agreements. In 1986,

Chernobyl's meltdown signaled a new level of international urgency.

## Citizenship in the Global World

Globalization has enriched some but left others far behind, who then turn to religious or nationalist ideals. Nation-states have also found their autonomy and influence compromised by increasing global integration. In some ways, international organizations have come to enjoy more clout in defining citizenship than even national governments—particularly in the Third World. Nevertheless, local differences continue to give the globe a strong element of diversity.

SUPRANATIONAL ORGANIZATIONS

International bodies have risen to facilitate global interaction, but they have also encroached on the autonomy of nation-states. The World Bank and International Monetary Fund are the most important world financial institutions, aiding development while exacting promised reforms from borrowing nations. Challenging dictatorial regimes in the 1970s and gaining support from major foundations, nongovernmental organizations (NGOs) emerged to promote various causes with funds and clout to rival those of national governments. Amnesty International, for example, grew from obscurity to become the world's most powerful human rights organization.

VIOLENCE

Fierce ethnically or religiously charged violence has also become a global concern. Violence of other sorts—natural disasters and poverty—affects billions. Competition and corruption has led to fierce outbreaks with regional, if not global, implications. Violence in Rwanda, for example, affected many countries in the region. Other societies, seeking healing and progress, have endeavored to investigate past abuses. "Truth" commissions, as seen in South Africa, not only legitimize democratic successors to oppressive regimes, they also aim to open the way for peace to blossom rather than vengeance. At the same time, however, in the Balkans, violence could only be halted through an escalation of warfare.

RELIGIOUS FOUNDATIONS OF POLITICS

As globalization spreads, religion has produced a way to redefine the nation-state and restore some of its autonomy. In India, Hindu nationalists claim that the secular state has trampled on the rights of the majority Hindu population by coddling the minority Muslims, and they insist on changes that would produce a moral community featuring a social hierarchy with themselves at the top. In the Islamic Middle East, critics of modernity assert Islam as a means of averting crass materialism and individualism. Khomeini's Iran is just one example. In the United States, fundamentalist Protestant groups also rally against secularization and many of the social changes arising since the 1960s.

DEMOCRACY

Democracy has spread largely due to new political and social movements and has become the standard political model for most world nations. China continues to resist, in spite of the great demonstrations for democratization bloodily crushed by government troops, as in Tiananmen Square in 1989. Government control of information has become increasingly difficult. Many individuals prefer to risk their lives getting smuggled out of their country for a chance at greater opportunities elsewhere. In Mexico, democracy finally triumphed after the Zapatistas rebelled against Mexico City and supranational forces and international news agencies intervened to change world opinion. Embarrassed, Mexico City decided to negotiate and set up elections that swept the ruling party from power.

## QUESTIONS FOR CLASS DISCUSSION

1. What were some of the major concerns that led to the breakup of the cold-war order?

2. What are some of the major "agents" of globalization? What stimulated their rise in importance? What drives their spread and success?

3. What are some of the features of the new global order today?

4. Why have supranational organizations risen to challenge the power of some nation-states?

5. Why has democracy become the political model employed by most of the world's nation-states?

## MULTIPLE-CHOICE QUESTIONS

1. Which of the following statements about global conditions at the beginning of the twenty-first century is *not* true?
   a. Large political empires that had dominated in the past had lost their influence.
   b. The cold war ceased to have any impact on global realities.
   c. The First World no longer existed.
   d. The Second World and its structures had collapsed.
   e. The Third World saw some nations becoming economically advanced while others did not.

2. Pressures that directly helped end the cold war included all *but* which of the following?
   a. ruinous regional wars such as those in Vietnam and Afghanistan
   b. enormous, unsustainable military budgets
   c. popular frustration with the Soviet economy because it could not supply basic commodities
   d. fervent beliefs that Communism was evil and had to be destroyed
   e. rising popular opposition to the use of nuclear weapons

3. Solidarity in Poland and Gorbechev's rule in the Soviet Union
   a. represented a resurgence of Communist power.
   b. represented the beginning of the end for Communist control in the Soviet Union.
   c. contributed to the escalation of the cold war.
   d. contributed to rising military tensions between the United States and the Soviet Union.
   e. had no impact on world events at all.

4. The *apartheid* system of South Africa sought most of all
   a. to raise the status of blacks in South Africa.
   b. to maintain the supremacy of the black-dominated government of South Africa.
   c. to raise the status of whites in South Africa.
   d. to maintain the supremacy of the white-dominated government of South Africa.
   e. to keep whites and blacks separate but equal.

5. Problems faced by decolonized Africa include all of the following *except*
   a. political leaders who cannot deliver on their promises.
   b. ethnic and religious rivalries between Africans themselves.
   c. civil wars and military coups.
   d. leadership practices which used political power to persecute rivals.
   e. the economic potential of Africa's vast quantities of natural resources.

6. What technological innovation greatly contributed to the globalization of finance in the late twentieth century?
   a. banks
   b. the Internet
   c. the IOU voucher
   d. multinational companies
   e. the balance transfer option on credit cards

7. Which of the following does *not* represent a major motivation behind migration?
   a. the lure of economic opportunity elsewhere
   b. the pressures of famine at home
   c. the chance to gain political freedoms
   d. the attractiveness of a foreign vacation
   e. the need to flee warfare and conflict

8. Many hoping to relocate are forced to languish in refugee camps while awaiting their chance to migrate. The majority of these refugees are found in which part of the globe?
   a. North America
   b. South America
   c. Europe
   d. Africa
   e. Asia

9. Which of the following is *not* a way that culture has been affected by globalization?
   a. It has eclipsed local cultural expressions that did not prove popular.
   b. It has allowed individual consumers, of music, for example, more options to choose from.
   c. It has contributed to the spread of local cultural expressions to broader audiences.
   d. It has led to the rise of new local cultural expressions inspired by foreign cultures.
   e. It has created a single, standard culture for all people everywhere.

10. In today's globalized world, the feature that most profoundly distinguishes rich and poor is one's access to
    a. knowledge and communications.
    b. oil and coal.
    c. stable government.
    d. international allies.
    e. TV and movies.

11. In wealthier nations, populations are
    a. growing rapidly because people can afford to have more children.
    b. shrinking because pollution has raised the mortality rates of children under six years of age.
    c. growing slowly or shrinking because the people of wealthier nations have fewer children.
    d. growing rapidly because health care has greatly improved the life expectancy of people.
    e. growing slowly because only a few people can afford health care.

12. Which statement about U.S. women is *not* true?
    a. One major effort by women's organizations has been to secure equal pay for equal work.
    b. Women get much fewer college degrees than men.
    c. Women still struggle to secure top management and administrative positions.
    d. Balancing child care and career is still a major issue.
    e. U.S. feminists have begun to play a stronger role on the global scene.

13. NGOs like Amnesty International
    a. have no impact on governments.
    b. have only a small impact on governments.
    c. exist solely to make money.
    d. enjoy significant influence, especially in the Third World, by shaping world opinion.
    e. concern themselves with local issues only.

14. Across the globe, secular governments have begun to face increasing pressure from religious fundamentalists that seek to redefine the "nation" in religious terms. Examples include all but
    a. Khomeini's Iran.
    b. Islamic terrorists.
    c. Hindu nationalists.
    d. conservative U.S. Protestant groups.
    e. hate groups like German skinheads.

15. Which major country has strongly resisted all calls to implement democracy even though much of the rest of the world has moved to embrace it?
    a. Russia
    b. India
    c. France
    d. China
    e. Panama

## MAP EXERCISE

Looking at a map of the globe, identify five major avenues of migration and explain what factors contributed to get people to leave their homes in great numbers.

## KEYWORDS

Cocama-Cocamilla
three-world order
Americanization
International Committee of the Red Cross
European Union
International Monetary Fund (IMF)
Sandinista coalition
"contra" rebels
Strategic Defense Initiative ("Star Wars")
Iron Curtain
KGB
Soviet bloc
Kremlin
Gdansk shipyard
Solidarity
"civil society"
Prague Spring
*apartheid*
African National Congress (ANC)

Boers
National Party
Communist Party of South Africa
Bank for International Settlements
"the debt crisis"
North American Free Trade Association (NAFTA)
Maastricht Treaty
European Union
"guestworkers"
MTV
rock videos
National Basketball Association
World Cup
World Soccer Federation (FIFA)
reggae
Bob Marley and the Wailers
"Latin" music
*boleros* (ballads)

Los Lobos
rap
hip-hop
Village People
"YMCA"
Silicon Valley
World Wide Web
Indian Institutes of
    Technology (ITT)
"pill"
Acquired Immune Deficiency
    Syndrome (AIDS)
Center for Disease Control
"gay cancer"
Mercosur free-trade pact
Fourth World Conference
    on Women
Non-Governmental
    Organizations (NGOs)
    Forum for Women

Organization of Petroleum
    Exporting Countries
    (OPEC)
Gulf War
acid rain
Earth Summit
"environmental miracle"
Chernobyl
supranational organizations
World Bank
Volta River Project
nongovernmental
    organizations (NGSs)
United Nations
Universal Declaration of
    Human Rights
"Magna Carta for
    Mankind"
Amnesty International
Ford Foundation

Hutus
Tutsi
United Nations Security
    Council
Rwanda's civil war
Truth and Reconciliation
    Commission

Hindutva (Hinduness)
Bhartiya Janat Party (BJP or
    Indian People's Party)
Tiananmen Square
Monument to the Heroes of
    the Revolution
Zapatistas

## ANSWERS TO MULTIPLE-CHOICE QUESTIONS

1. c
2. d
3. b
4. d
5. e
6. b
7. d
8. d

9. e
10. a
11. c
12. b
13. d
14. e
15. d

# Epilogue, 2000–The Present

- To assess the first seven years of the twenty-first century

## OUTLINE, CHRONOLOGY, AND SUMMARY

The twenty-first century brought with it the hope that peace and prosperity would prevail, but that, sadly, has not been the case.

## The United State, the European Union, and Japan

The attacks of September 11, 2001, on the United States ushered in policies pursuing "homeland security" domestically and "war on terror" internationally. After destroying the Taliban regime in Afghanistan, the United States toppled Saddam Hussein's regime in Iraq. Since those military campaigns, however, insurgency and other problems have divided U.S. opinion and generated rifts with U.S. allies.

Europe, meanwhile, showed increasing integration via the European Union. Falling European birthrates have stimulated the immigration of millions of Muslims. Immigration also affects the United States, but most newcomers there are from Asia and Latin America. Japan's low fertility and aging population have also attracted immigrants.

In Europe, political reactions against immigration have been sharp, especially in areas with high unemployment and especially against Muslims. Cultural clashes and terrorist activities in Holland, France, and Spain have raised questions about whether or not Muslims can be assimilated, prompting calls for government intervention.

## Russia, China, and India

As evidenced by outsourcing, some high-paying jobs can be performed anywhere in the world for any company in the world. The economies of Russia, China, and India are all growing steadily within the world market system. Russia's political system, however, has shown signs of heavy-handed executive branch control.

China has quashed political liberalization but allowed full economic liberalization. Although full entry into the global capitalist economy has been a success, problems such as environmental degradation, social imbalances, and so forth continue to challenge the Chinese state. Hosting the Olympics in 2008, China will signal its capacity to challenge the United States as a new superpower.

Indian economic success has been tainted somewhat by tensions between Muslims and Hindus. Economic growth has combined with Hindu nationalism, producing ugly episodes of violence between the two religious groups and political parties such as the BJP gaining advantage. Tensions between India and Pakistan have also been high, especially as both nations have developed nuclear weapons.

## The Middle East, Africa, and Latin America

Enduring signs of peace and prosperity are hardest to find here. The Middle East's dysfunctional societies and governments and Islamic extremists produce more problems than seem possible to solve, as the United States is discovering in Iraq. When elections are held, they often support radical parties. Terrible poverty combined with enormous oil wealth generates alienation and support for extremism or for nuclear parity as seen in Iran.

Africa faces the same pressures, in addition to the devastating consequences of poverty and AIDS. While some notable accomplishments, as in South Africa, have been achieved, many of Africa's latest events have involved ethnic cleansing, civil strife, and genocide.

Latin America's twenty-first century, by contrast, has been far less frightening. Globalization has made the wealthy wealthier. The poor, on the other hand, have often had to migrate or face unemployment and displacement. Politics has responded with the rise of leftist governments decrying U.S. influence and globalization in general.

## Conclusion

Presently, global warming and terrorism seem to be the preeminent international concerns.